Loving
YOUR
HUSBAND
WELL

Also by Lisa Jacobson

Loving

YOUR

HUSBAND

WELL

A 52-WEEK DEVOTIONAL
FOR THE DEEPER, RICHER MARRIAGE
YOU DESIRE

LISA JACOBSON

Revell
a division of Baker Publishing Group
Grand Rapids, Michigan

Published by Revell
a division of Baker Publishing Group
PO Box 6287, Grand Rapids, MI 49516-6287
www.revellbooks.com

Printed in the United States of America

Library of Congress Cataloging-in-Publication Data
Names: Jacobson, Lisa, author.
Title: Loving your husband well : a 52-week devotional for the deeper, richer marriage you desire / Lisa Jacobson.
Description: Grand Rapids, MI : Revell, a division of Baker Publishing Group, [2022]
Identifiers: LCCN 2022006279 | ISBN 9780800742423 (casebound) | ISBN 9780800736675 (paperback) | ISBN 9781493426720 (ebook)
Subjects: LCSH: Wives—Religious life—Miscellanea. | Marriage—Religious aspects—Christianity—Miscellanea. | Husbands—Psychology—Miscellanea.
Classification: LCC BV4528.15 .J34 2022 | DDC 248.8/435—dc23/eng/20220321
LC record available at https://lccn.loc.gov/2022006279

This publication is intended to provide helpful and informative material on the subjects addressed. Readers should consult their personal health professionals before adopting any of the suggestions in this book or drawing inferences from it. The author and publisher expressly disclaim responsibility for any adverse effects arising from the use or application of the information contained in this book.

Baker Publishing Group publications use paper produced from sustainable forestry practices and post-consumer waste whenever possible.

22 23 24 25 26 27 28   7 6 5 4 3 2 1

For Matt:
Truly, I have found him *whom my soul loves*—
holding on and never letting go of you.

Contents

Contents

Contents

Introduction

My friend, I can hardly wait for you to dive into this marriage devotional with me.

I feel I can call you *friend* throughout this book because, even though we may not have yet met, we share so much in common. Perhaps you find that hard to believe at first—with our different personalities, life experiences, or marriage dynamics—but I think you'll find over time that it's true. Just the fact that you picked up this devotional shows that we share a strong desire to grow in our faith and to deepen our marriages—and what a beautiful place for a friendship to begin!

Getting Started

So, as we're well on our way to becoming good friends, are you ready to get started?

Before we get too far, one of the first things I want you to know is that *Loving Your Husband Well* is intended to be read in tandem with your husband. That is to say, you can go through this devotional while he is reading the companion one, *Loving Your Wife Well*, written by my husband, Matt Jacobson.

It's not that you need to read your devotionals simultaneously or even on the same day (although that would be fantastic if you could make it happen!). Instead, the central point is that you'll both be focusing on the same Scripture verse, though each in our preferred translations, and the same biblical theme every week over the year together.

However, I should also add that while the theme will be identical in both devotionals, the content will not be. That's because Matt is writing to men from his perspective as a husband, while I am approaching it from my perspective as a wife. Same topic and verse, different angle.

"Okay, but what if my husband isn't interested in or refuses to read his devotional?" I can already hear many of you asking. Let me encourage you if that's your situation: Even so, you can benefit greatly and grow tremendously on your own. Yes, *ideally* you would go through these devotionals together, but it is not *essential*. You can carry on, trusting God to continue to do His work in your husband and in your marriage while you concentrate on what He has for you to do and grow in.

Ready to Dive Into Your Devotional?

For some of you, the idea of regular devotions might be new. If so, you'll probably want to think through the practicalities of this commitment, such as what time of day might work best in your current season of life.

For me, now that my children are older, I set my alarm in order to wake early enough to have thirty minutes or so to quietly study the Word and pray before our home begins buzzing with the noises of our teenage boys and our daughter who has special needs. However, when our children were younger, I waited until the afternoon for quiet time, when the little ones were either napping or resting. I also have night-owl friends who prefer the late evening to dive into their devotions.

So, whether you decide on morning, afternoon, or night, the main thing is to schedule your devotions at a time when you can be most consistent in showing up and to peacefully focus on what lies before you.

Now, as to what you'll need for those twenty to thirty minutes: All that's necessary are this devotional, a Bible, and a notebook (or some way to keep notes—I hesitate to suggest using your laptop or smartphone because they can be very distracting). I also recommend spending a few minutes in prayer before you even open your book, asking God to soften your heart and grant wisdom as you start your study.

About This Devotional

Next, whether reading the devotional along with your husband or on your own, you're going to want to pick a specific day— maybe on Sunday night or every Monday morning—to set aside time to read that week's devotion in its entirety.

Then throughout the rest of the week, you'll have your devotional time to study further, reflect on the week's theme, look up related verses, consider how to specifically apply the principle, and pray for God's purposes to be revealed.

You'll find that each devotion is divided into five parts: the week's theme and accompanying Scripture passage, followed by an introduction and short study of the topic, a few reflection questions, application suggestions, and a closing prayer.

The introduction and study: Every week, we'll take a closer look at that week's topic—ranging from joy and kindness to trials and covenant—to see what God's Word has to say on the subject. And before long, you'll likely notice my love for language, as we occasionally dip into the Greek to learn the meaning of some words, discovering the layers and complexities that will help illuminate our study. But don't worry if Greek isn't your thing; it's just a bonus if you're interested!

Reflection questions: While it might be tempting to quickly pass over these questions and get on to the application, I truly hope you'll take time to ponder what's being asked. Even if the questions feel awkward or convicting, please don't skip over them; think of them as an important, if uncomfortable, part of the growing process.

Application: Although I suggest several ways you might apply the week's theme, I also recognize that your personality and marriage dynamics will be unique to *you* and *yours*. So this is an opportunity to consider your relationship with your husband and what is most needed—and what the Holy Spirit impresses upon your heart and situation.

Prayer: You'll find a short prayer at the end of each devotion, but let's think of it as merely a starting point. Your Heavenly Father wants to hear from you, so freely pour out your heart and desires before Him.

Disclaimers: Lastly, you'll come across some disclaimers throughout this devotional. As Matt and I have spent several decades in marriage ministry and marriage coaching, we are keenly aware of and deeply concerned for anyone in a potentially abusive marriage relationship. We encourage you to seek professional, wise, biblical help and protection if this is your situation.

Please Join Me

And now, friend, I hope you'll join me in this rich, yearlong journey of learning to love your husband well. I believe we have much to look forward to in the coming weeks and months: further spiritual growth, greater wisdom, better understanding, and a deeper love than ever before. So let's get started!

1

Love

Beloved, let us love one another, for love is from God, and whoever loves has been born of God and knows God. Anyone who does not love does not know God, because God is love.

1 John 4:7–8

My husband, Matt, and I met at a small dinner party in Portland, Oregon, on a Friday night. But it wasn't until the following Thursday afternoon that we decided to get married.

Although some people considered this shockingly fast (my parents, for instance), I found those six days to be some of the slowest of my life. I couldn't see why it was taking Matt so long to realize I was "the one" when I knew it the minute he entered the room. *Obviously*, we were made for each other. So it remains a mystery why it took him three days to reach the same conclusion—and yet another three days to get around to telling me.

But, thankfully, before that first week was out and, more importantly, before I flew back down to Southern California, we were both talking marriage. And it seemed the most natural conversation in the world at the time. This life-changing chat took place on that last day together, after he and I had taken off for a glorious afternoon hike up the pine ridge. We suddenly found ourselves standing face-to-face, only inches apart. I looked up into his beautiful blue eyes and breathlessly wondered what would happen next. And that's when Matt leaned down for our first clumsy, teeth-clunking kiss.

Once we stopped laughing over that most awkward moment, he reached for my hand, and we started to walk back down the old logging trail toward our car. But before we got far, Matt stopped, turned to me, and soberly asked, "You know what this means, don't you?"

"Yes, I do," I answered matter-of-factly. "We're getting married." As if this kind of thing commonly occurred in my twenty-six years of single life.

It's possible I'd watched too many Hallmark movies, but that's honestly how the conversation went. And we really did marry only a few months later.

What's strange to me, though, is how I can vividly remember every detail of that initial Friday night dinner right up until the memorable kiss on Thursday afternoon—and yet I can't recall when we finally got around to saying "I love you." Funny that we'd discuss such a big decision like marriage before declaring our love for each other, don't you think?

But you'll be glad to hear that we eventually exchanged those three momentous words and have since repeated them thousands of times over our three decades of marriage. However, I should add that it wasn't until we were well into our married life that we even began to grasp what *love*—true, sacrificial, biblical love—means.

The love I'm referring to is the *agapē* love spoken of in the Bible—that laying-down-your-life, putting-others'-interests-first kind of love. It's the one so poetically and powerfully described in the "Love Chapter" of the Bible, 1 Corinthians 13.

Love is patient and kind; love does not envy or boast; it is not arrogant or rude. It does not insist on its own way; it is not irritable or resentful; it does not rejoice at wrongdoing, but rejoices with the truth. Love bears all things, believes all things, hopes all things, endures all things. (1 Cor. 13:4–7)

As lyrical as this passage is, if you've been married for any length of time, you've already discovered love is much easier—and more pleasant—to read about than to *live out*. And, at times, it can feel nearly unattainable. Almost unreachable.

Yet be encouraged: As we grow in Christ, it *is* possible to enjoy a deep and abiding 1 Corinthians love—by His grace and in His strength.

So maybe your story doesn't include a six-day romance, or maybe you haven't been married for thirty years. Whatever your story, this I do know: God loves you, unconditionally and perfectly, and He is *for* your marriage. And I can't wait for us to share more in the coming devotions about how that love is wonderfully woven together throughout His Word.

My friend, this is only the beginning of His beautiful love story for you.

Reflection

- What is your definition of *love*? How does it match up with the description found in 1 Corinthians 13?
- How do you think your husband would answer if asked the ways he feels loved by you?

Application

How do you say "I love you" to your husband not only in the words you say but in the choices you make? Consider writing out 1 Corinthians 13:4–7, and brainstorm three specific ways you can express love according to this biblical passage. Just keep in mind that this short "assignment" is intended to inspire and encourage you, not to overwhelm you. In the weeks and months to come, we will be walking through many, if not all, of these attributes listed in 1 Corinthians 13.

And if you're interested in studying other verses that talk about *agapē* love, here are but a handful of them:

- "But God shows his love for us in that while we were still sinners, Christ died for us" (Rom. 5:8).
- "A new commandment I give to you, that you love one another: just as I have loved you, you also are to love one another. By this all people will know that you are my disciples, if you have love for one another" (John 13:34–35).
- "Greater love has no one than this, that someone lay down his life for his friends" (John 15:13).
- "Beloved, let us love one another, for love is from God, and whoever loves has been born of God and knows God" (1 John 4:7).

Prayer

Dear Heavenly Father, I want to thank You for loving me so much that You sent Your only Son to die for my sins (John 3:16). I'm nearly overwhelmed by Your deep and abiding love for me. This year, I want to grow in my love for my husband—not only in how I feel about him but in the things I say and do, as well as the choices I make. In Jesus's name, amen.

2

Priority

Therefore a man shall leave his father and mother and hold fast to his wife, and the two shall become one flesh.

Ephesians 5:31

I held my breath, waiting to hear how our oldest son might answer the question. Now that he was in his twenties and a man on his own, as a parent, I couldn't help but wonder what the reply would be.

The question he was asked went something like this: "What part of your childhood contributed the most to the strong faith you have now?"

My mind immediately raced through some of the possibilities he might mention: his Christian upbringing, education, good friends, or faith community. But he named none of these influences. Instead, he stated simply, "It's the way my parents loved each other—that's probably what has impacted me more than anything."

Our love. Of all things.

Not that we have parented perfectly (because we haven't) or that we're perfect Christians (we're not), but that, by God's grace, two imperfect people have heavily invested in a loving relationship with one another. And what a difference it's made.

Now, if you're a parent and currently in that intensive season of raising young children, this idea of investing in your marriage might feel daunting—or downright impossible. I can almost hear the protest: "But our kids *need* us. It's not that I don't love my husband; I don't see how I can, or *should*, push them aside for our marriage!" As it stands, you hardly have enough hours in the day to get it all done, let alone add another significant investment of time and intention.

And I hear that. But if you love your children (and I know you do!), I want to encourage you that one of the greatest gifts you can give them is a strong marriage.

Besides, I'd argue that investing in a close relationship doesn't take *away* from your kids, rather the opposite: It will give them a sense of security and a warm, happy environment to grow up in. As a loving, affectionate couple, you will inevitably bring joy into the home, which in turn will pour over onto the rest of the family.

I can say that with confidence as our grown kids are quite vocal about how they *love* the way we love each other. They've told us, and they've told their friends. It means the world to them to know we're not merely committed but we genuinely enjoy one another. Because when they see us kiss, talk kindly, laugh aloud, sneak away together—then we're not only showering love on each other; we're showering love on *them* too.

But it's more than beneficial to your kids; it's also biblical. God describes you and your husband as "one flesh" (Eph. 5:31), and that is no mere euphemism for sex. It is referring to a one-flesh closeness that's not found in any other relationship besides marriage. And, as you can imagine, it takes a significant amount of time and attention to develop such a deep level of intimacy.

So, if you love your kids and want the best for them, as counter-intuitive as it may feel right now, don't be too quick to give them *everything* or *your all*. Save some of your (preferably premium) time and energy for their dad, and you'll find that love flows over onto your children in more ways than you could've guessed.

And if you don't have children, or if they're grown and gone, then consider if there's anything else that competes with your marriage. Maybe it's your work or church commitments or personal hobbies or some other interest. While I'm sure these are all fine and worthy endeavors, it's your marriage relationship that comes first.

Reflection

- Do you consider your marriage your top priority? Or do the kids (or other commitments) come first in your heart and your schedule?
- What do you think your husband might say if asked where he falls on your list of priorities?

Application

Take out your calendar or planner and look at the time you have set aside to spend with your husband (and, sorry, but children's events and family activities don't count for this one). Do you have daily moments that are dedicated for the two of you together? A weekly date night of some kind? A weekend ritual where it's just you two? If not, then do what you can to make at least one of those happen, even if it means cutting back on other regular activities.

And if your children protest about doing stuff without them? If they complain that you're not including them in this conversation or inviting them to that fun event? Simply smile and, without apology, explain that you and Daddy love each other—*and them*—and that is why you're enjoying this special time.

Prayer

Dear Lord, You designed my husband and me to be "one," and yet, You're also aware of the heavy demands on my time and attention. Please help me see how I can make my marriage my priority so we can enjoy true oneness and so our children (or friends and family) will enjoy the blessing of seeing two people who love each other deeply. In Jesus's name, amen.

3

Faith

> But without faith it is impossible to please Him, for he who comes to God must believe that He is, and that He is a rewarder of those who diligently seek Him.
>
> Hebrews 11:6 NKJV

Not everyone remembers the exact moment they came to faith in Christ. But I do. And although I was relatively young—*too young*, some people said—and with very little Bible knowledge, I made a clear and conscious decision to follow Jesus. *No turning back.*

As an eager seven-year-old, I found the Christian faith to be new and inviting. My parents had only started going to church (regularly, at least) the year before, yet I could already see the change in their lives and feel the difference in our home. My parents had become born-again believers, and I wanted that too—not out of childish impulse, as you might think—but out of a genuine desire to know and love Christ.

Yes, I was young and familiar with only a dozen or so Bible verses, but I had memorized John 3:16, like every good child in Mrs. Allen's first-grade Sunday school class. "For God so loved the world that He gave His only begotten Son, that whoever believes in Him should not perish but have everlasting life" (NKJV). And I believed that with all my heart.

So, what about you? If you're a Christian, do you recall when you decided to follow Jesus? Was it one specific moment or more of a journey? Maybe you made the decision as a child, like me, or maybe you were radically saved as an adult, like Matt's parents. Perhaps you have never wavered in your faith, or you may have slowly slipped away over the past few years or more. And if that second one is more your story? Take heart: God is always ready to forgive anyone who repents and gladly welcomes anyone who seeks Him. "If we confess our sins, he is faithful and just to forgive us our sins and to cleanse us from all unrighteousness" (1 John 1:9).

But whether you're new to the Christian faith, recently re-committed, or have been a believer for decades—wherever you're at in your walk with God—He promises to draw near to you if you draw near to Him (James 4:8). So, friend, I hope you'll draw near.

And if you don't know how to draw near to God? Or if you desire to grow in your faith but don't know where to begin? The Christian faith is not as hard or complicated as we tend to make it. You don't have to join a women's Bible study, nor must you attend the adult Sunday school class or a small group (although you might enjoy any of these). It's not required that you have hour-long devotions in the morning or stay for second service at church. As a follower of Christ, the main thing is to love and obey Him according to His Word. Daily walking in faith with Him, one step at a time.

Now, you might be asking, "But what about my husband and *his* faith? And what about our marriage?" Because that's probably why you picked up this *marriage* devotional—to grow in faith together or to grow *back* together.

And I have two responses to those (very legitimate) questions. The first is something you likely already know: You are not responsible for your husband's faith. You can influence him, and you can encourage him—but you cannot make choices for him.

Then, in response to that second question, I believe there is nothing better you can do for your marriage than grow in your own faith. Although it might not feel all that powerful or effective at first, you will find that it is both over time. Your thriving faith and godly obedience will inevitably flow over into your marriage relationship.

So, I encourage you to focus on Christ—trust Him to work in and through you—and then watch what He does for your marriage.

Reflection

- Do you remember when you decided to follow Christ? And do you walk closely with Him now?
- How about your husband? Where is he in his faith? What role does faith play in your marriage?

Application

If you've never written out your personal testimony of how you came to faith, why not work on that this week? Include as many details as you can remember and the various people or circumstances God used to help bring you to Christ.

Then spend time over the next few days reflecting on what it means to be a woman of faith. Not only what it generally means for a Christian but what you specifically want to see in your own life. Maybe do a short search on "faith" in the Bible, looking up passages such as Romans 10:17; Ephesians 2:8–9; and Hebrews 11:1–2, 6. Then write out what you learn through your study.

Prayer

Dear Heavenly Father, I want to draw near to You and grow in faith. My deepest desire is to walk closely with You. Help me to follow You, and I pray the same for my husband. In Jesus's name, amen.

4

Healing

He heals the brokenhearted
and binds up their wounds.
Psalm 147:3

have forgiven the unforgivable."

She whispered those few words to me over a cup of coffee at our small kitchen table. No context. No conversation. And yet there was something about her quick, short statement that made my soul shudder.

I had no idea what my mother-in-law could have possibly meant, and I'll admit I was tempted to press her for the details. *What? What did you forgive? And, please, what happened to you back then?* Not merely because I was curious but because I had a hunch it would help explain why Mom was the way she was and why she didn't let anyone get too close to her. I would know; I had been trying my best for over twenty years. This sentence was the nearest to being open I'd ever experienced from her, and I quietly guarded it as a precious gift.

That one statement, such a mystery.

I later asked Matt if he knew what his mother could've been referring to. If he had any guesses what "the unforgivable" could have been. He didn't. Mom rarely talked about her childhood, and most of her stories took place after she had married Dad. Other than her tales of caring for two baby bear cubs as a young girl, her growing-up years were a bit of a blank.

In some ways, I wish they would have remained a blank and that we had never learned why she whispered what she did. But toward the end of her life, Mom finally confided in Matt about the awful things done to her. She told him about the family members who had assaulted her as a young girl, about the kinds of things that should never, ever happen to the helpless and innocent.

About *the unforgivable.*

And yet, after all the wrong done, Mom later welcomed those same family members into her home. She cooked up pot roast and potatoes and poured countless cups of hot coffee. Then she and Dad shared the gospel with them over a second piece of her homemade apple pie.

Can you even imagine? No, neither can I.

But then again, maybe you *can* imagine. You might even be able to relate. And if so, I'm grieved to think such wrongs were done to you. Or you may have suffered other hurts or harms: neglect, abandonment, loss, or devastation. How many of us quietly walk around with the deepest of wounds.

And then, whether we intend to or not, we bring those wounds into our marriage.

So now, can I gently speak to you as a Christian sister as well as an older married woman? I believe with all my heart that God is a Healer and a Redeemer. That He can lovingly mend your broken heart and heal those tender wounds over time and often with the help of a wise, professional counselor.

I say this in faith but also because I've witnessed miraculous healing with my own eyes. In addition to my dear mother-in-law, I have several close friends who have endured *the unforgivable* and by God's help and healing touch have gone on to enjoy safe, loving relationships with their husbands. And I will pray the same for you.

Then let me also add this: If you've ever been seriously hurt or wronged, I would urge you to share your wounds with your husband. How it grieves me to think of my mother-in-law keeping that pain to herself all those years. No one should ever have to carry such a thing alone.

Above all, I hope you turn to Jesus. He is your Wounded Savior, and He is able—more than able—to deliver you.

Reflection

- What kind of wounds did you bring into your marriage—emotional, physical, spiritual, or relational? And what about your husband's wounds?
- Have you talked about your woundedness with your husband? Have you ever discussed any of his?

Application

Next, I want to encourage you to search the Word for God's help and spiritual healing. Steep yourself in the many beautiful Scriptures on healing and the Healer over the next few weeks, maybe months. Here are but a few to begin:

- "O LORD my God, I cried to you for help, and you have healed me" (Ps. 30:2).
- "But he was pierced for our transgressions; he was crushed for our iniquities; upon him was the chastisement that brought us peace, and with his wounds we are healed" (Isa. 53:5).
- "He himself bore our sins in his body on the tree, that we might die to sin and live to righteousness. By his wounds you have been healed" (1 Pet. 2:24).

You might want to reserve an entire page in your notebook for such Scriptures and others that distinctly speak to you. Maybe pick out one or two verses to memorize so you always have them tucked in your heart.

Prayer

Dear Heavenly Father, only You know the depth of my pain and desire for true healing. Please touch my body and heal my heart wounds. Help me in my distress. In Jesus's name, amen.

Note: If you still carry deep wounds from the past and haven't already done so, I strongly suggest you seek out a biblical, professional counselor for further help and insight. Ask a trusted friend or mentor, perhaps someone in church leadership, for a referral or recommendation.

5

Affirmation

Let each of us please his neighbor for his good, to build him up.

Romans 15:2

As I suspected, he was already sleeping. I slipped from the couch and out to the front porch to read my new book late on a Sunday afternoon. It wasn't unusual for my pastor-husband to drift off after we'd returned from a full day of church, especially since he'd been up early going over his message, and I didn't want to risk waking him.

So I crept out the front door and curled up in the old wicker chair with my mom's fall-colored quilt thrown across my lap to keep me warm in the October breeze. But I'd hardly reached page seven of my book before Matt joined me and sat in the companion chair next to mine.

He didn't appear rested or very peaceful—not like I'd expect to find him after the pleasant day of fellowship we'd just enjoyed. No, if I were to describe his state of mind right then, I might have chosen language like "discouraged," "downcast," or "disheartened." Nor was this confined to that one particular day; the heaviness that hung about him had been building for some time.

Now, no one likes to picture a pastor in a place where he's contemplating "quitting," and yet, for a fearful minute, I wondered if that was the word he had dared to whisper to himself while inside and clearly *not* napping.

Oh, and if only you could've heard him preach on that marvelous Sunday! He had delivered a particularly compelling message from 1 Corinthians—one that stayed with me throughout that lovely autumn afternoon. Truly inspiring. And although it hadn't occurred to me to mention it earlier, it seemed like this might be a good time to tell him.

So, pretending not to have noticed my husband's heavy sigh, I remarked on how much I benefited from the morning's sermon. He glanced up and looked at me questioningly, which I took as my cue to continue. From there, I listed off many of the qualities I admired about him but hadn't gotten around to communicating. For instance, how I found him an uncommonly effective preacher—clear, engaging, insightful—as well as a rare combination of both truthful and compassionate.

He drank in my admiration like a man who had gone far too long without water. Well, who would've thought? Is it not *obvious* he's a gifted teacher? And, even if he could use some affirmation, wouldn't he prefer hearing it from the church body instead of his wife?

But I was mistaken. He needed to hear it from *me*—the woman in his life.

And so that afternoon brought yet another revelation. Up until then, I believed self-doubt and discouragement were my own personal specialty. I had no clue my husband would be vulnerable to the same kinds of take-down messages that I wrestled with. He'd always given the impression he was in charge and confident. *So self-assured.*

I hadn't realized how desperate his thoughts ran when no one was watching. How he sometimes doubted whether his ministry really mattered or whether he was actually making a difference. It turns out he needs to hear *my* voice—a loving, loyal, encouraging one—to drown out the defeating voices that tend to swirl around in his head.

Maybe this will surprise you, or perhaps you're already aware, but my husband is not the only one. That man of yours needs to hear encouraging, affirming words from you every bit as much as mine needs to hear them from me. He wants to know he's important and valued and that he's not failing in your eyes.

Just don't wait until he's whispering the word *quit*. Speak encouraging words of affirmation to him. Because these, my friend, are life-giving words to the man who needs to hear them.

Reflection

- Are you being purposeful in how you use the power of your words?
- Do you speak words to encourage and build up? Or have careless words had a negative impact on your marriage?

Application

Speaking words of affirmation might be unfamiliar territory for you, and just the thought of it might make you feel awkward or uncomfortable. Maybe you didn't grow up in a home in which people spoke so openly, so kindly, but don't let that keep you from building up your husband with the words you say.

If you are new to this practice, you might want to begin by writing out those qualities you appreciate or admire about him. Be as precise as possible. For example, you can use phrases such as these:

- "I appreciate how you _____."
- "You're such a good dad to our kids when you _____."
- "I see how hard you work at _____."

And for more suggestions, I recommend my book *100 Words of Affirmation Your Husband Needs to Hear* as a good resource (along with the companion book written by my husband, *100 Words of Affirmation Your Wife Needs to Hear*).

Prayer

Dear Lord, I want to speak encouragement, strength, and life into the heart of my husband. Help me to use my words wisely and lovingly. Show me how I can build him up in You. In Jesus's name, amen.

6

Spiritual Warfare

> Finally, be strong in the Lord and in the strength of his might. Put on the whole armor of God, that you may be able to stand against the schemes of the devil. For we do not wrestle against flesh and blood, but against the rulers, against the authorities, against the cosmic powers over this present darkness, against the spiritual forces of evil in the heavenly places.
>
> Ephesians 6:10–12

You've changed, Lisa. You're not the same person you were before you left."

That was my mother's observation after I'd returned from spending several months studying and traveling in the Middle East. She said I walked differently, acted differently, even *looked* different.

And as much as I wanted to deny it—to insist I was the same young woman as before I left—I knew what she meant. My time in the Middle East *had* changed me. I was more serious and less naïve. More wary and less trusting. But I was also stronger and wiser because of that challenging experience.

Whether I meant for it to happen or not, my time in the Middle East had visibly impacted my entire demeanor and how I viewed the world around me. From then on, when I walked into a public place, I entered on guard, watchful for any threat or potentially dangerous situation. If alone, I scanned the area for an emergency exit or a nearby security officer who might help if called. I carried Mace in my purse and always parked my car in a well-lit spot. I was on alert and vigilant.

While I don't often talk about what happened that summer I spent in the Middle East, when I do open up and share, people ask if I regret having gone. But I don't regret the trip despite what I've been through.

And here's one of the reasons why. Although I encountered several dangerously close calls and one genuine threat, I also came to see that I am "strong in the Lord" and not as defenseless as I might have first believed. I don't have to be a helpless victim; I can actively guard myself—and so can you.

I'm no longer talking about the Middle East here but about you and your marriage.

Not that I'm equating marriage with a war zone, but then again, spiritually speaking, it's not too far off the mark. Our spiritual enemy is not likely to leave our marriages alone, and we should be ready to take a stand. Just take a look at the above passage in Ephesians 6, where we're instructed "to stand against the schemes of the devil" (v. 11) and warned that we wrestle "against the spiritual forces of evil" (v. 12). Otherwise stated, as believers, we need to be battle-ready: This is war.

Perhaps you prefer not to think of your marriage as a spiritual battleground. Admittedly, it's not the most romantic picture, and yet there's no avoiding the reality of it. Friend, we must face that we have a powerful enemy—one who would be all too happy to harm your marriage, ultimately destroying it if possible. And, as unpleasant as it is to consider, I would rather be aware and prepared than caught off guard, wouldn't you?

To prepare for this battle, the Bible instructs us to put on the full armor of God and to stand our ground (Eph. 6:13). Further down, this passage then describes the many pieces of spiritual armor available to us: the belt of truth, the breastplate of righteousness, the shoes of readiness, the shield of faith, the helmet of salvation, and the sword of the Spirit (vv. 14–17).

This passage in Ephesians 6 is a call to action! And we can't risk waiting until the trouble or danger is here before getting serious about spiritual warfare. So pick up your sword, friends. God gave us His Word not only as a source of hope and encouragement but also to equip us against the deceitful lies and traps of the Enemy.

Open that Bible on your bedside stand. Read, meditate, memorize, and study it. You'll never be the same again if you do.

Reflection

- Do you recognize that you have an enemy in your marriage (and that it's not your husband)?
- What are you actively doing to protect your marriage from and prepare it for spiritual warfare?

Application

As you prepare for battle, pull out your notebook and list the various pieces of spiritual armor God has for you. Then, next to each one, write out what it might practically look like in your marriage. For instance, try taking up "the sword of the Spirit"

(v. 17). Consider starting each day by reading His Word and perhaps memorizing key passages to refute the devil's lies that sometimes haunt or tempt you.

And if you're interested in learning more about spiritual warfare, here are a few more verses to get you started: 2 Corinthians 10:3–5; James 4:7; and 1 Peter 5:8. Although this is a somewhat sobering study, we must never forget it's God "who gives us the victory through our Lord Jesus Christ" (1 Cor. 15:57). He is our Overcomer!

Prayer

Dear Lord, help me to remember that my husband and I have an enemy and that it's not each other. I pray that You will protect our marriage, but also that I'd take up the armor You've given so I can fight for our marriage. In Jesus's name, amen.

7

Laughter

A time to weep, and *a time to laugh*;
a time to mourn, and a time to dance.
Ecclesiastes 3:4

I believe there are two types of people in this world: those who like plenty of pillows and those who do not. I would fall into that first category. My husband, on the other hand, would be in the second one. And I should tell you right now that this matter of pillow-collecting has been a source of disagreement our entire marriage—one of the few important issues to divide us.

But, thankfully, as *the manager of our home* (can you hear how biblical that sounds?), I get to decide on the pillow situation. So piles and piles of pillows it is. If you ever make it to our home, you'll find them scattered across nearly every couch and chair and stacked up high on the bed we share. My motto is, *You can never have too many pillows.*

Now, if you're reading this and starting to feel sorry for my poor, pillow-loathing husband, please don't. Because, trust me, he has his way of getting back at me.

Most every night, as I cross the bedroom floor to crawl into my cozy bed, Matt will start pitching pillows at me as if we were at the state fair, and this was one of those carnival games where you have the chance to win a giant stuffed panda. I've tried to tell him this is extremely immature behavior, and we're far too old for such games, but he refuses to listen—especially since I can't stop giggling, no matter how many thousands of times we've played this silly game. It's ridiculous.

But it's also rather sweet. Because no matter what our day has held or what we've been through, we usually end our day on a happy note of laughter.

Our older kids, who are now grown and moved away, have since informed us that this is one of their favorite memories growing up—the sound of Dad and Mom laughing at bedtime. While it's not anything I was aware of back then, it's rather fun to hear now. They've even shared that no matter what was going on in their lives, all seemed right with the world when they listened to our laughter late into the night.

Perhaps there's not a lot of laughing in your marriage. You're too busy, too stressed, or simply too solemn. If that's you, then you might be interested in the number of Bible verses that mention laughter as something tremendously beneficial in your life. It's true. Here are just a few of them:

- "All the days of the afflicted are evil, *but the cheerful of heart has a continual feast*" (Prov. 15:15).
- "*A joyful heart is good medicine*, but a crushed spirit dries up the bones" (Prov. 17:22).
- "A time to weep, and *a time to laugh*; a time to mourn, and a time to dance" (Eccles. 3:4).

Now, I'm not suggesting everyone have a pillow fight before retiring for the night, but you might want to *seriously* consider how you can bring more fun and laughter into your lives. And whatever you do, don't wait until all the problems are solved or all the trials are over; who knows when that will be, and besides, those are often the times when you *most* need the healing effects of a good laugh together.

So, can I encourage you to bring laughter back into your relationship? Tell a joke, play a prank, or do something a little silly. Start a water fight or throw a pile of pillows. You might be surprised how good it feels to laugh again and enjoy the lighter side of life.

Reflection

- Is there much laughter in your marriage? Why or why not?
- What kinds of things make you laugh when you're together? What is something your husband would consider fun or funny?

Application

For some of you, this will be an easy assignment to carry out; for others, however, this will be one of the more awkward ones. But even if you have a naturally somber personality, you can still initiate and enjoy some fun and laughter.

Get out your notebook and write as many ideas as you can, such as telling a knock-knock joke, greeting him with a water balloon, determining to laugh at *his* jokes, trying out your best pun, or playfully teasing or clowning around. I think you'll find that laughter truly is the best medicine.

Prayer

Dear Lord, You have made laughter a gift for us to enjoy and a balm for our souls. Make our home a place of laughter and our marriage a relationship known for its joy. Help me to remember to laugh and lighten the hearts around me, starting with my husband's. In Jesus's name, amen.

8

Trust

Trust in the Lord with all your heart,
    and do not lean on your own understanding.
In all your ways acknowledge him,
    and he will make straight your paths.

Proverbs 3:5–6

Our first fight was nearly as memorable as our first kiss. Maybe even more so. Matt and I enjoyed such a smooth engagement period that it never occurred to me that it might ever be otherwise. At the time, I couldn't even imagine what there could be to "fight" about, still less that we'd have a situation go from zero to sixty in under twenty minutes.

His zero, my sixty.

But one mid-June afternoon, a couple of months before our wedding day, I cheerily walked into his apartment and set down my purse on the kitchen counter when my eye caught sight of an airline ticket to California tucked under a pile of mail.

My fiancé is leaving me. One glance at that United Airlines ticket, and I knew it. I'm not saying it was logical, but that's where my mind went, and my husband-to-be was about to see a side of me he'd never seen before.

Filled with fear and panic, I angrily lashed out at him with a myriad of irrational questions and accusations: "What is this ticket for?" "Where are you going?" And more to the point, "Why would you be leaving me?"

Matt tried to calm me down by explaining that it was simply a ticket to a good friend's graduation. He'd forgotten to tell me, but he'd be flying out on the following Friday and would only be gone for a few days.

At that point, I corrected Matt, informing him that, no, actually, he *wouldn't* be flying anywhere. I see now that it must have sounded a lot like an order, but what he didn't understand was that it was more of a heart cry. *Please don't leave me. I'm scared you won't come back.*

Matt was initially confused by my angry response to his plans for California, but this particular tactic—this I'll-tell-you-what-you-will-and-won't-do approach—only made my fiancé raise his eyebrows and dig in all the deeper. Back and forth we went until we were at a total impasse for the first time in our relationship. In the past, we'd always managed to work things out or come up with a reasonable compromise. But how does one "meet in the middle" when the issue is a flight to California? You either go, or you *don't* go.

And so our argument continued to escalate, with me becoming increasingly irate. Then, suddenly, without saying a word, Matt whipped around and went into the back bedroom, shutting the door behind him and leaving me standing there alone. Stubbornly, I stood in the same spot, tearfully waiting for him to return so we could finish fighting this thing out.

But he stayed in the room such a long time that I concluded he wasn't coming back—not *ever*. I was now truly convinced he was leaving me, just as I'd suspected all along. At last, unable to take it, I silently cracked open the door, confident I'd catch him packing his bags for his departure.

But I called it wrong.

Neither packing nor leaving, that man of mine was kneeling by the side of the bed and *praying*. I could hear him pouring out his heart—and our terrible argument—before the Lord as if it was the most natural thing in the world. My fiancé was trusting God with our problems. What a wild way of resolving an otherwise irreconcilable situation!

Although I'd prayed about many things in my twenty-six years, I'd never thought to pray about an argument, anger, or hurt feelings. I had always considered those kinds of issues to be my own to work out. Now I knew differently, and this knowledge rocked my world. What a beautiful realization that I could trust God with my husband, our marriage, and, yes, even our conflicts.

And so can you. Did you know that it doesn't always come down to you to figure things out or solve problems? Instead, you, too, can take it to the Lord in prayer, trusting Him to guide you and care for you. Even when your situation—or relationship—seems utterly impossible, you can entrust it to His loving, almighty hands.

Trust in the Lord with all your heart.

Reflection

- Are you trusting the Lord with the "impossible" in your marriage? With the state of your current relationship? With your future?
- What is one area in your marriage that God is asking you to trust Him with today?

Application

Trust is a big topic found in the Bible—whom we're to put our trust in and why. So if you struggle with trusting, why not spend some time this week meditating on what Scripture says, including the many verses found in the book of Psalms.

- "When I am afraid, I put my trust in you. In God, whose word I praise, in God I trust; I shall not be afraid" (Ps. 56:3–4).
- See also Psalms 9:10; 40:4; and 118:8.

Prayer

Dear Lord, I confess that I have not always trusted You with my marriage. But I want to spend more time praying about my fears and concerns and less time fretting over them. Give me a heart to trust You, Lord, with my life and love. In Jesus's name, amen.

9

Joy

May the God of hope fill you with all joy and peace in believing, so that by the power of the Holy Spirit you may abound in hope.

Romans 15:13

Certain compliments stick with you. So when one of our wedding guests described me as the most joyful bride she'd ever seen, I knew I'd remember her words for a long time. And I have, even thirty years later. To be called *joyful*—well, that's better than *beautiful*, *bright*, *sexy*, or any other word that comes to mind.

Even better than *happy*. After all, happiness is only something that *happens* to you, but joy? Joy is something you *choose*.

I started to see this distinction before Matt and I ever celebrated our first wedding anniversary. Because, in less than a year, I went from enjoying the happiest season of my life to experiencing the greatest sadness I had known up until then. Just like that, my world came crashing down in less than twenty-four hours.

Still blissful newlyweds, Matt and I had been traveling around Europe for an extended business trip when I had a hunch something was different with me—different *inside* of me. Initially, I kept my suspicions secret. Several weeks went by, and then, unable to keep it to myself—or to keep my breakfast down—I whispered the exciting news to Matt.

We were expecting a baby, and we were both *over the moon!*

Understandably, we were eager to tell the whole world, but there we were, far from home with only a handful of newly acquainted friends with whom to share our big news. Nevertheless, we made fun plans to announce it around our host's breakfast table the following morning.

Except we never got that chance.

I was awakened in the night by a sharp pain that jolted me out of bed. As I stumbled around in the darkness, I immediately sensed something was very wrong. Trying not to awaken Matt, I made my way to the small bathroom down the hall, flipped on the light, and realized I'd begun to bleed.

Although I'd not experienced a miscarriage before, I instinctively understood what this was—the beginning of an end. That's all I could think; it's all I could see. And I wept loudly as I watched my hopes and dreams drain down in the middle of the night in some strange house outside of Paris.

> Weeping may tarry for the night,
> but joy comes with the morning. (Ps. 30:5)

Maybe this seems an unusual choice of story to share in a chapter on joy. Admittedly, I could've mentioned other brighter moments—such as the evening Matt kissed me under the Eiffel Tower or the memorable walk down the Champs-Élysées—yet that would be saying more about happiness than joy.

Joy is about weeping at night but then wiping away your tears in the morning. It's about trusting God in the dark while waiting for the sun to come out again. It's about staying steady no matter what is going on around you because you know—personally, intimately, powerfully—the Source of all real joy.

> You make known to me the path of life;
> in your presence there is fullness of joy;
> at your right hand are pleasures forevermore. (Ps. 16:11)

The beautiful thing about joy, and what differentiates it from happiness, is that it doesn't depend on our circumstances, feelings, or another person—not even your husband or child. Such dependence is an unrealistic expectation. And it's also an unfair burden to put on one person, no matter how much they may love you and desire for you to be happy.

Instead, joy is something tucked deep down inside you that nothing and no one can take away from you. Joy is found in having faith that God knows your heaviest heartache and your wildest dreams and then trusting that He is working all things together for your good (Rom. 8:28).

While it didn't appear possible in my sorrow, I eventually found joy again, even after that heartbreaking miscarriage. Oh, not right away; it took months for me to physically heal and longer still before I began to hope again. But slowly, over time, I began to see some good things come out of that tragic loss—unexpected things, like how my heart became increasingly tender for the Lord and how Matt and I grew closer after experiencing that grief together.

So, friend, you may weep in the night, but I pray you'll find joy in the morning. We have an invitation to draw near to God, whatever our situation, and a choice to be grateful for all that is good. I hope you will choose joy—in your life and your marriage.

Reflection

- What would you say brings you joy? Are you struggling to find joy in your life right now?
- In what ways would you like to bring more joy into your marriage?

Application

Name one way you can choose joy this week. Maybe it's something you'll decide to be grateful for, or maybe it's a wish or a regret you're going to let go of and count on God to care for. Consider memorizing a verse (or a song) about the joy of the Lord. Recite it, or sing it, every day of this coming week.

Here is but a small selection of verses on joy that you can choose to meditate on: Psalm 16:11; John 16:24; Romans 12:12; 15:13; Philippians 4:4; and James 1:2.

Prayer

Dear Lord, I know You are the Source of true joy, and I long to be filled with the joy that only You can bring! Help me to choose joy in my marriage, no matter my circumstances, frustrations, or disappointments. In Jesus's name, amen.

10

Like-Minded

Finally, all of you *be of one mind*, having compassion for one another; love as brothers, be tenderhearted, be courteous.

1 Peter 3:8 NKJV

Little did I know when Matt plopped that flat of Oregon berries on the kitchen counter during our first year of marriage that this would be an exchange we'd refer back to in the years, even decades, to follow. He had picked up the tray of fruit at a local roadside stand on the way home, and you can be sure I was full of newlywed appreciation for his thoughtfulness.

So that evening we enjoyed fresh berries and cream for dessert, and I found myself grabbing a handful whenever I passed by the flat over the next day or two. How indulgent to devour so many beautiful berries whenever I wanted!

Although I might have found the flat of berries beautiful, Matt didn't appear to be quite as pleased. Much to my bewilderment, he became increasingly irritable over the next few days until, at last, he couldn't stand it a minute longer. He finally came out with it: "I don't get it. Why aren't you putting up the berries?"

"Putting up the berries?" I looked at him blankly.

Confused, I looked around the kitchen to see where he expected me to "put up" the flat. On top of the fridge? On a high shelf? I was truly at a loss as to what he could be talking about.

His irritation then turned to total frustration, bordering on anger. "*Put up the berries*. You know, make jam, freeze them, or something!"

I must have looked as baffled as before because then Matt went on to explain that where he grew up in Oregon and northern British Columbia, Canada, if someone in the family brought home a flat of berries, his mom would immediately *put up* the berries, as in prepare them for the winter months.

Oh. I see.

Except that's not how it worked in the Southern California suburb I grew up in. I'd never heard of "putting up" fruit (which he had a hard time believing, but it's the truth!), and we never worried about the winter months by those warm, sandy beaches. It's not that I was being difficult or contrary, only that I came into this marriage with a different experience and set of expectations—and you might even say a different vocabulary.

So that was the moment we both looked at each other and realized we had a lot more learning to do if we were to "be of one mind."

Perhaps you've experienced a similar moment in your marriage. Or maybe quite a few of them. That moment when you both stood there looking at each other, wondering what the other person was possibly thinking, doing, or even saying and then what it was going to take for you to get on the same page.

You are not alone. Rarely, if ever, do two people instantly and easily become of one mind. It takes time, attention, and patience for a couple to grow like-minded. Without meaning to, we often *assume* the other person knows us—what we want, how we feel, or where we're coming from—and is either being uncaring or selfishly ignoring our interests. But that's not always the case. Often, it's more a matter of learning to understand—and appreciate—one another.

While there are many ways to grow in your understanding—by observing, listening, and reflecting—one of the best ways to learn about your spouse is by simply starting a conversation. If it's unclear what he is thinking (or why), ask him about it. Then be willing to share your thoughts and experiences as well. You'll also want to assume the best about each other rather than jumping to conclusions, being mindful of when they're based on your personal background or triggers.

Yes, it takes time and work to "be of one mind," but I believe you'll be glad you put in the effort in the years to come. Only yesterday Matt brought in a large bucket of grapes from his grapevines growing out back, and I just had to laugh. Time to put up the berries. Although this time, thirty years later, he didn't need to say a word because I knew what he meant by now. I've learned to speak his language, and he mine.

Reflection

- Would you say you and your husband are like-minded? Why or why not?
- What is an area in which you'd like to be more like-minded with him?

Application

If you're hoping to be more of one mind with your husband, ask questions that show your interest: "What are you thinking?" "Why do you think that way?" "What is your background or experience with this?" and then, "Would you like to hear what is going on in my mind?"

Ideally, this conversation would take place over a cup of coffee or a tall glass of iced tea and at a time when you're both relatively relaxed and rested. And remember, your intention is not to prove a point but to get to know each other better and get one step closer to your desire to be like-minded.

Prayer

Dear Lord, I know Your desire is for us to "be of one mind," so help us to grow closer in both heart and mind in our marriage. Please give us a better and deeper understanding of one another. In Jesus's name, amen.

11

Delight

Behold, you are beautiful, my beloved, truly delightful.

Song of Solomon 1:16

I genuinely blushed when I first read the Song of Solomon. As a young teen girl, I could hardly believe they would let a sensuous book like that make it into the Bible. It didn't seem appropriate and bordered on shocking. But there it was: "Let him kiss me with the kisses of his mouth" (1:2), or my husband's favorite (or at least the one he most teases me about), "Your two breasts are like two fawns" (7:3).

Honestly, Mr. Jacobson!

So yes, it wasn't until I was older and a married woman that I began to fully appreciate the beautiful romance played out in the Song of Solomon. Now that I'm well past a blushing age, I love how this biblical love story begins with the Shulammite woman expressing her sheer pleasure and joy in her lover. She unashamedly tells him, "For your love is better than wine" (1:2), and then a little later in the first chapter, "Behold, you are beautiful, my beloved, truly *delightful*" (v. 16). In case you haven't picked up on it yet, these two are terribly in love.

And everything is going very well with the two lovebirds until further on, when we get to chapter 3. Then this same woman falls asleep and experiences a rather vivid and terrible dream—a nightmare, really. And in this dream, she looks for her lover all over the city but can't find him anywhere. You can practically feel her fright when he's nowhere to be found.

In her search, the woman finally comes across the night watchmen and anxiously asks if they have seen him anywhere. The situation is beginning to feel hopeless when suddenly, she spots her man in the distance and races to meet him. Rejoicing to be reunited with her love, she declares to anyone who will listen, "I found him whom my soul loves. I held him, and would not let him go" (3:4).

Maybe this is "only" a dream, but can't you picture their warm reunion? Imagine her teary relief and the joy of their embrace? *Sheer delight.*

This is the kind of delight that real lovers enjoy—whether they've been married one year or fifty. Now, maybe we haven't been married for fifty years, but my good friends John and Susan have, and I'll never forget the first time Susan invited me to their home for lunch. She welcomed me in the door, and only a minute later, Pastor John came in behind me and walked straight over to his lovely wife. And there, the two of them kissed—right on the lips!

Not a mere peck, mind you, but a kiss lasting for several seconds. In the middle of the day. In front of this new guest. And oh my. What a visible demonstration of *delight* between two people married for more than five decades! I'd never seen anything like it, but I knew then that's what I wanted for the rest of our days too.

So, how about you and your marriage? How do you express *delight* in your husband (and vice versa)? Do you light up when you spot him in the distance or when he comes home from work (or when you do)? Hold on to him and never want to let go? Maybe kiss him on the lips for a few seconds or more?

Or perhaps that's not where things are at right now.

It's not just you. We're all prone to forget the lover's delight once we've been married for a while. We get wrapped up in our frustrations and lost in the busyness of everyday life rather than getting wrapped up in his strong arms and lost in our love. But, oh friend, don't miss out on showing delight in the one whom your soul loves. Like a Shulammite lover, hold on and don't ever let him go.

Reflection

- What is the level of *delight* in your marriage?
- How might you, as his lover, express delight for your man?

Application

Consider the look on your face, the tone of your voice, and the words you say to your husband. Do you communicate to him (and anyone else who happens to be around), "I found him whom my soul loves" (3:4)? If so, how do you show him your delight? And if not, what would you say is holding you back?

Next, bring out your notebook and write out the many different ways you could express delight in your husband. Get as specific as possible. For example, *I want to smile warmly when he walks in the door.* Or, *I'm going to use my "sweet" voice more often when speaking to him.* Or perhaps, *I'm going to go all out and wrap my arms around him, whispering in his ear, "Your love is better than wine."* Have a little fun and see if you can make *him* blush!

Prayer

Dear Lord, thank You for this man, the one whom my soul loves. *I regret that we've fallen into a bit of a rut, but I want to remind him (and myself) that he is my one true love. Renew my delight in my husband and help me to express it in ways that would be meaningful to us both. In Jesus's name, amen.*

12

Respect

Honor everyone. Love the brotherhood. Fear God. Honor the emperor.

1 Peter 2:17

I've always heard it said that women long for love and men wish for respect. Pastors and conference speakers make this remark as if stating the obvious—similar to "the sun sets in the west." Such a clear statement of fact that no one would consider debating it.

Women need love; men need respect. Plain and simple.

So you can imagine my bewilderment when this whole love and respect thing became an apparent issue in our marriage. Oh, it wasn't the love part; we did reasonably well in that department. Instead, it was the matter of respect that brought the most hurt and confusion. And even anger.

Because when I feel disrespected? Flames follow.

However, as young marrieds, it took us a while to identify the reason behind these flare-ups. We'd address each occurrence as an individual event—not realizing these incidents all shared a common theme—and inevitably leave our discussions feeling like the other person was way out of line. Matt believed I was overreacting, and yet I couldn't seem to get a grip on my exaggerated response to these relatively minor situations.

It would go something like this: I'd be chatting with a group of friends, recounting some past family escapade, when Matt would correct me on a little detail. Right in the middle of my story. Annoying and unnecessary.

Or, perhaps I'd tell the kids "no dessert" and announce early bedtime that night. Then in would waltz Matt holding a carton of strawberry ice cream, cheerfully declaring he'd start reading aloud the rest of *Hank the Cowdog*. Fun Dad wins.

So, maybe it sounds silly for a grown woman to flip out over a small correct-the-detail moment. And it's not the end of the world that the children enjoyed a treat while listening to their father read an entertaining book late into the evening. Yet there I was—very much a grown-up—inwardly resenting Matt's revisions to my story or begrudging the entire time he was reading about Hank's hilarious adventures on the ranch.

For me, it wasn't about getting tiny details right or exactly what time the kids went to bed—it was about *respect*. Or what I perceived as a lack thereof.

That's when I felt compelled to look more closely at the biblical teaching on respect. As it turns out, respect is *not* limited to "what men need." For example, in 1 Peter 2:17, we're instructed to "honor everyone." The word translated as "honor" here is *timaō* in the Greek—a word that means "to value" or "to revere."[1] You'll often see it translated as "respect" in this verse or, as it's put in the Berean Study Bible, "Treat everyone with high regard." And where it says "everyone"? As you might've guessed, that word means *everyone*.

So, this goes to show that the need for respect is universal and not really silly at all. You could even say it's biblical. And maybe my two small examples here don't mean much to you, but you probably have your own—those things that communicate respect (or *disrespect*) to you. Naturally, you want to feel loved, but you also want to feel *honored*—especially by the man you married.

Now, some of you have been quietly nodding your heads throughout this discussion, while others have been cheering more loudly. But before we break into applause, let's return to that *honor everyone*. Because, even though I've made a case that this absolutely includes you as a wife, it most assuredly applies to your husband too.

Because "they" weren't wrong about this part—your man does need respect. He desires that you *show* him respect. I emphasize *show* because I've heard from too many wives who *felt* respect for their husbands . . . but didn't necessarily *show* it—at least not in a way that was meaningful to them.

For instance, consider how you respond to your husband's decision-making; your reaction speaks volumes. Is your first impulse to question him? Challenge him? Or do you communicate respect for his choices and judgment in the discussion that follows?

Or reflect on how you talk *to* him—and *about* him. Do you speak respectfully (as you want him to speak to you)? Do you talk honorably about him to your friends and family? Your tone and your words are two powerful ways to communicate respect.

And if you haven't shown respect to your husband, why not recognize that mistake, ask forgiveness, and start anew? Enjoy the blessing of a marriage built on the strength of mutual respect.

Reflection

- Do you feel respected in your marriage? Is there a loving way you can communicate your need for respect from your husband?
- Do you think he would say that he felt respected by you if you asked?

Application

Respect is typically communicated by what you say, what you do, and how you treat the other person. Think of three to five things that say "respect" to you, and be as specific as possible. Then find a good time to (respectfully) share your list with your husband. Just be ready to hear what sorts of things make him feel respected by you as well.

Better yet, find out his list first and take to heart what he shares with you. Then make it your mission not merely to have respect for him but to *show it* in unmistakable ways.

Prayer

Dear Lord, I desire for there to be mutual respect in our marriage. Please help me to show respect for my husband with what I say and how I treat him. And help me to lovingly communicate my need for respect as well. In Jesus's name, amen.

13

Humility

Yes, all of you be submissive to one another, and *be clothed with humility*, for

"God resists the proud,
But gives grace to the humble."

1 Peter 5:5 NKJV

Aggressively helpful." That's how our daughter put it. This is exactly how she describes herself. When I first heard her say it, I stared at her for a few seconds, somewhat incredulous that there was an actual term for this kind of thing.

Part of me wanted to pretend I didn't understand what she meant by the unusual expression. And yet, that wouldn't be true. I knew full well what she was talking about. Our daughter is highly competent, among her many other fine qualities. She's one of those who instinctively knows where things go and what to do next. She's naturally very efficient and makes sure things are done right.

And, without a doubt, helpfulness is an admirable virtue. I mean, what could be better than a woman who perceives what needs to be done and how to do it? It's a power-packed gift.

Except our conversation wasn't over. Because then my still-single daughter lamented, "We laugh about it now, Mom, this tendency I have to be a tad overly helpful. But I want to be anything—*anything*—but a controlling wife."

I wasn't laughing now. Because the (humbling) truth is that I have this same inclination, this same ability to be "aggressively helpful." I don't mean to boast, but I can show my husband the fastest route to Costco, inform him of the best way to spend our Saturday, and handily instruct him on how to repair the water heater (after googling it). I already know what the man is trying to say and, if he pauses long enough, will jump in to finish his sentence if necessary.

As you can see, I can be very, *very* helpful.

Oh, and you too?

But how does this "gift" actually play out in our marriage? Is it truly helpful, or is it merely a thin disguise for control? Because, rather than a blessing, you'll find that this "rightness" tends to be slowly destructive—whether your motives are pure or not. I know it's easy to excuse our aggressive actions under the pretense that it's for the greater good. Faster, smarter, better, wiser—who can argue with that?

Yet what we've convinced ourselves is helpful is, in reality, rooted in pride. *I'm the one who knows what is right, best, and brilliant. I am up here, and you are . . . somewhere below that.*

Oh friend, the Bible is filled with cautions against the pitfalls of pride. For example, in the book of Proverbs, we're told, "When pride comes, then comes disgrace" (11:2) and "One's pride will bring him [or her] low" (29:23). Disgrace, destruction, and lowliness: Those are what await the woman who operates in arrogance.

But there's an encouraging option too. It's called *humility*. Just take a look at what Proverbs says about the person who chooses humility: "With the humble is wisdom" (11:2), and the person "who is lowly in spirit will obtain honor" (29:3). Wisdom, honor, and blessing: Those are what come to the woman who walks in humility.

Now, I can almost hear some of you asking, "But what if I *am* right? And I *do* know the best way to get to the store or to fix the water heater?" No one is telling you not to pass on that very helpful information or assist in that important project—*if* offered in the spirit of humility. It's when we *insist* we're the one who knows the most or does it best that it becomes a problem.

And if you're not sure where you are on this matter? Try taking this short quiz: Ask yourself, *Am I willing—happy even—to take my husband's preferred route to our destination . . . even if it takes ten minutes longer? And, Am I content to let him work on that task, in his own way and in his own time, without all of my good advice?*

Hopefully, you answered yes to both. Because a humble person knows, down to the deepest part of her soul, that she is *not* always right and that she *doesn't* always know best. And even if she is technically correct, she cares more about loving the other person and doing what's kind to him than she does about being right.

Enjoy the honor and grace of one who walks in humility.

Reflection

- Am I genuinely being helpful in my marriage? Do I walk in humility?

- Or do I tend to be that always-knows-best, controlling wife?

Application

Reflect on what it might mean to be "clothed with humility." What would humility look like on you? Maybe put together a short list of your "humble clothing." What would this wardrobe consist of? And where would you wear it? Be as specific as possible, given your own personality tendencies and marriage dynamics.

Prayer

Dear Heavenly Father, I desire to dress in the beauty of humility. Reveal where I might be controlling and prideful and not as "helpful" as I'd like to think. Please help me to walk humbly with my God (Mic. 6:8). In Jesus's name, amen.

14

Friendship

One with many friends may be harmed,
but there is a friend who stays closer than a
brother.

Proverbs 18:24 CSB

wish I could take the credit and say it was intentional. That
we knew full well what we'd be building when we started our
lovely morning tradition. But in all honesty, it was probably as
much due to a love for coffee as it was a love for each other—at
least in the beginning.

Even before our wedding day, on most mornings Matt and
I would meet over at Java Bay Café across the street from his
apartment to enjoy a strong cup of Pacific Northwest coffee.
There we'd talk about our dreams, ideas, fears, concerns, wedding plans, and just about everything else on the planet. So it
seemed only natural to continue on with the practice once we
were married.

And this is why every morning for over thirty years now, Matt and I have started the day by sharing a cup of coffee together. It's always the same: a pot of French press, fresh-ground medium-roast coffee beans, raw sugar crystals (for me), and cream (also for me), all carried in on a serving tray. It's our slow and sweet Jacobson tradition.

But it's what follows the pour that's my favorite part. We spend the next thirty minutes to an hour talking together—discussing everything from the creative ways we could remodel the kitchen to current events in the news to quotes from an interesting book or funny movie. And yes, we sooner or later talk over the plans for the day and who is going where or doing what, but we try to keep that to a minimum.

Here is what we *don't* do during our morning coffee: We don't use this time to solve problems, work out differences, discuss finances, or troubleshoot. That is what business partners do and, although we *do* run a business together, this sacred time is primarily reserved for *friendship* and *friendly topics*.

Maybe we didn't start this tradition with a purpose in mind, but over time it's become one of those secret ingredients for our loving marriage and friendship. And here's why: If you haven't noticed or experienced it yourself, it's far too easy for a married couple—no matter how in love they are on their wedding day—to find themselves operating more and more like coworkers, coparents, or cohabitants over the years. Possibly all three.

And yet while it might be a normal slide and in some ways a necessary one, who gets married with the hope of becoming functional teammates? Personally, I was looking for something more. I was looking for a lover and a friend, and I'm almost certain you were too.

Which brings us right back to coffee. Not that you have to drink coffee, but purpose to set aside time (daily, if possible!) to enjoy each other as *people*, not limiting yourselves to "dad and mom" or "cook and cleaner" or even "manager and chauffeur." You're loving companions too, remember? So consider the kinds of things that friends do—talk, laugh, joke, reminisce, discuss—and then be sure to make space for that sweetness in your life.

If you haven't already, start investing in a strong friendship together—the kind that can carry you through every season of your life.

Reflection

- What kinds of topics and activities did you and your husband enjoy as friends in the earlier years of your relationship?
- In what ways would you like to see your friendship deepen with him now?

Application

Maybe morning coffee doesn't work for your marriage or schedule, but what is a time that could be set aside to intentionally build your friendship with your husband? In the evening after the kids are in bed? The lunch hour? Or perhaps a weekend ritual would work best for you. Then schedule the time, but be sure to communicate expectations as to what this time is going to be and what it will *not* be.

Also, while Matt and I enjoy *talking* together over coffee, it might be that you and your husband enjoy adventure or sports or projects as something else that means *friendship* to you (or him). Be willing to get creative, but try to be consistent too. Make it a priority to do the kinds of things that lifelong friends do.

Prayer

Dear Lord, I desire to be close friends with my husband and not merely coworkers in life together. Show me how I can be a good friend to him and how we can deepen our friendship even in the season we're currently in. In Jesus's name, amen.

15

Peace

You keep him in perfect peace
whose mind is stayed on you,
because he trusts in you.
Isaiah 26:3

I immediately recognized her gorgeous smile through the stained glass of our front door, and yet I stood there for another half a minute or more, slightly mortified to see her standing outside on our porch. This relatively new friend had dropped by unannounced, and you wouldn't believe how *utterly* unprepared for visitors I was that afternoon.

Looking back, I have only myself to blame, as I was the one who so cavalierly tossed out, "Stop by anytime!" when I'd bumped into her in town a few weeks earlier. This woman had only recently become a new client of my husband's, and she also happened to be a former national beauty pageant winner and bestselling author. I guess it never occurred to me that she'd actually take me up on my friendly offer.

Now here we had none other than Ms. USA waiting outside our door on a warm Wednesday afternoon. So what else could I do but invite her inside?

I tried to imagine what might be going through her mind when she entered our home, only to find our young sons casually rollerblading past her through the living room on their way outside. Then I cringed when I spotted the small mound of dirty socks the kids had piled into a corner by the entryway, not to mention the thick layer of Central Oregon dust on the piano that had inspired some child to write her name in it. Now, I had explanations for all those things (except maybe that pile of socks) but nothing worth going into at that moment.

Our client-friend said she intended to stay only a few minutes, but once I got over my initial embarrassment (and pushed aside the clean laundry I'd been folding on the couch), we soon became lost in conversation. The "short" visit stretched out to nearly an hour. However, after a while, she realized the time, and we walked together over to the door to say our goodbyes.

And that's where she stopped. With one hand on the door handle, she turned around to say one last thing before leaving. "You know, there's something about your home . . ." She hesitated as if searching for the right words.

Here it comes, I thought, and I could feel my face flush. *She's about to comment on the crazy state of things around here.*

But I was wrong. Instead, she finished her statement with, "I feel it's so full of peace here."

She spoke as if she never noticed the rollerblading boys, the stockpile of wadded-up socks, or the impressive collection of dust bunnies. None of that appeared to register with her. For some reason, where I saw noise, mess, and mayhem—she saw life and peace.

Now, how can that be? How can anyone describe a home as peaceful when you've got kids skating through the living room? Those were the questions I asked my husband as we turned out the lights later that night.

And here was his answer to me: "Lisa, don't you get it? It's more about relationships than rooms. You could spend all day cleaning and it might make things tidier, but it doesn't necessarily bring about peace. *Peace starts with us.*"

I could see he was onto something.

He was speaking of the peace that starts in your heart, spills over into your relationships, and then spreads throughout your home. The peace that begins with Christ *in* you. It's the tranquility you can enjoy no matter what you're facing or what your day holds.

And this is the beautiful *peace* talked about in the Bible—so much more than a mere absence of conflict. Biblical peace remains unruffled by circumstances or situations because it doesn't depend on what's happening around us or to us. This peace is quietly tucked down in the deepest part of our hearts.

So how do you create this kind of peace in your home and marriage—not only with relatively small things, like unexpected company and a somewhat disheveled house, but with the bigger challenges and setbacks too?

The short answer isn't as complicated as you'd think. You start by setting your eyes on Christ and trusting Him, whatever else may be swirling around you. The Bible promises "perfect peace" to those who keep their minds steadfastly fixed on Him and take refuge in Him.

> You keep him in perfect peace
> whose mind is stayed on you,
> because he trusts in you. (Isa. 26:3)

Reflection

- What would you say is the level of peace in your home? And what about in your marriage?
- Does the peace of Christ "rule in your hearts" (Col. 3:15)?

Application

Rather than focusing on all the things that might be "wrong" with your house or husband, consider how you can contribute to the peace of your home—the peace that starts in your heart. Maybe memorize Isaiah 26:3, and then recite it whenever you start to feel troubled or distressed.

Prayer

Dear Heavenly Father, I long for peace in my marriage and home. Please reveal anything in me or about me that might be compromising that peace. I want the peace of Christ to rule in my heart, as Your Word says, and for that peace to fill our home. In Jesus's name, amen.

16

Asking Forgiveness

Confess your trespasses to one another, and pray for one another, that you may be healed.

James 5:16 NKJV

You wouldn't think that ordering pizza for our sons could be such an offense. But believe me, I was offended, and I think you'll understand better when I tell you why.

Matt and I were heading out to meet friends for dinner on a Friday night, so I instructed our youngest sons, ages fifteen and sixteen, to cook up the hamburger in the refrigerator for their dinner. I even started to give detailed instructions on how to season and fry the meat, but our sixteen-year-old stopped me with his "C'mon, Mom, you've got to be kidding me" look. He had it handled.

And apparently, all was well in dinner world.

That is until I mentioned to their dad in the car that I'd left the boys to make their own supper. True, they don't have much experience in the kitchen (that's what happens when you have two parents who enjoy cooking!), but what a perfect time to begin. However, Matt wasn't as optimistic. He expressed concern that the boys wouldn't feel "cared for" being left on their own like that. But I assured him they would be just fine, adding that I felt it would be an opportunity for them to grow in their skills.

So you can imagine my surprise when we returned home from our double date to find three big pizza boxes on the kitchen island. How odd! It wasn't like the boys to spend (their own) money on pizza when we had perfectly good food in the fridge. Or, more to the point, when we'd had a short but clear conversation about cooking up the hamburger for dinner.

And that's when I discovered Matt had texted the boys to go ahead and order pizza instead.

Now, if you're suspecting this underhanded move made me mad, you'd be mistaken. I wasn't mad—I was *furious*. Because while the mature woman in me understood there are worse things than boys ordering pizza, the betrayed girl inside me viewed this as downright treason.

But why would Matt uncharacteristically go around me in this way? A legitimate question that later launched an emotional discussion that went late into the night. This was when I learned that while grown-up Matt believed our sons capable of cooking hamburger, the young boy inside him was concerned we were sadly neglecting our children—as he sometimes felt neglected as a child.

So this wasn't really about the boys or me; it was about him and old, unhealed wounds.

Matt and I have come to call these moments "triggers"—when something is said or done that sets off an out-of-proportion response based on our childhood experiences or hurts. We're not speaking as therapists or counselors; we're merely saying this as a couple who have encountered such situations multiple times in our marriage.

We each have our own set of triggers. He has his, and I have mine. Because, wouldn't you know it, this pizza-text incident set off a whole different set of alarms for me. The behind-the-back communication. The disrespect. The fun dad over the mean mom. Talk about *triggers*!

So, how did we resolve this small yet significant disagreement? First off, we talked it over together, each listening as the other explained what was in our hearts and minds at the time. Then Matt acknowledged he had wronged me. Yes, he had an understandable, even sympathetic, explanation, but it wasn't an excuse. Neither did he settle for saying "I'm sorry"—an inadequate response where there's been a real offense—but he also humbly asked my forgiveness.

We take that "extra" step beyond a basic apology because, as believers, we're called to *ask* forgiveness, as well as to grant it. Most of us would agree that it's one thing to throw out an easy "I'm sorry" but quite another to put yourself in the position of begging or humbly requesting forgiveness. Yet, it's this humbling step that can bring about true healing and sweet reconciliation.

If you're not in the habit of asking forgiveness when you've sinned or offended your spouse, I encourage you to start now. And there's no need to make a fuss over it; all that is necessary is to sincerely say the words, "Will you forgive me for [state the offense]?" Then it's up to the offended party to forgive and let it go (but more on that next week).

Reflection

- Are you aware of your husband's "triggers"? Of your own?
- Do you practice asking forgiveness in your marriage?

Application

Can you think of anything you've said or done recently (or not so recently) that you know was offensive or hurtful to your husband? Do more than apologize—ask him to forgive you, specifically naming what it was that you did. Something like, "Will you forgive me for when I said *such and such* or did *this or that*?" Then wait humbly for his answer, keeping in mind that he might not respond immediately or as you hope.

Here I'll add, if you share my own tendencies, don't soften your question with excuses or bring up what he's also done wrong. Instead, you'll want to save your explanations for another time (if truly necessary and helpful) and any confrontations for a different discussion.

Prayer

Dear Heavenly Father, I want to work on my side of our marriage. Help me to identify my wrongs in our relationship and then to humbly ask his forgiveness for them. Please soften his heart toward me so that we can walk together in the freedom of forgiveness. In Jesus's name, amen.

17

Granting Forgiveness

Bearing with one another and, if one has a complaint against another, forgiving each other; as the Lord has forgiven you, so you also must forgive.

Colossians 3:13

Remember that notorious, sneaky pizza text? The one where Matt went around my explicit instructions to our sons and messaged them that they could order pizza rather than cook up the hamburger at home as I'd asked? Yes, *that one*. And how hurt and offended I was by this blatant end run by my very own husband? Then you'll also recall how we eventually worked it out, wrapping up a difficult conversation with a neat and tidy ending in which he sincerely asked my forgiveness.

Except that's not the end of the story.

Because, as I'm sure you know, there are two parts to the forgiveness process: First, there's the *asking* by the offender, and then there's the *granting* by the offended. And what's more, just as the offended cannot make the offender ask for forgiveness, neither can the offender make the offended forgive him. Each party has a decision to make about how they'll respond to the offensive situation. To forgive or not to forgive.

And, as it happens, I tend to be a *slow forgiver*.

I can't explain it, but something inside me fiercely wants to hold on to the offense, even after my husband has apologized and asked my forgiveness. As though I'm concerned he'll get away too easily with his wrongdoing. Or maybe it's that I want to make sure he's very, *very* sorry. Or perhaps I want him to suffer a little longer for his (albeit repented) sin.

Simply put, I have struggled to embrace true forgiveness as it's found in a loving, biblical relationship. And you, too, may share my struggle in this.

Before we go any further, let's take a closer look at the definition of *forgive* in the Bible. The Greek word is *charizomai*, meaning, "to grant as a favor" or "to pardon or rescue" or "to freely give."[1] *Rescue*—that's a fascinating concept to consider, isn't it?

And do you know what else stands out to me? The definition of *forgive* doesn't say anything about whether the other person, the offender, *deserves* to be forgiven or not. In fact, it implies the very opposite, that it is *undeserved*. Not unlike how we didn't deserve the forgiveness we've freely received from God our Father through Christ Jesus (Eph. 4:32).

So when we reflect on how we've been mercifully rescued, pardoned from our sins, and redeemed by the blood of the Lamb, we are in no position to hang on to an offense or exact further payment. God's Word is abundantly clear on how we are to respond to anyone, husband or otherwise, who is genuinely seeking our forgiveness. We are called to forgive as we've been so freely forgiven.

Last, I want to say a word to whoever might be looking at my recent sneaky-pizza-text incident and agonizing because you only *wish* your hurts were this small. Oh friend, I am so very sorry. I realize there are some hurts and offenses where forgiveness feels beyond what anyone could, or even s*hould*, be able to bear. The wound is too severe and the pain too searing to even consider it.

And to be sure: Left to yourself, forgiveness would be impossible. It's only when we look at what Christ has done—laid down His very life for us—that we can, in turn, find it possible to grant forgiveness to others. By His grace alone.

You have held on to your suffering long enough, dear friend, and I hope you can lay down right now this painful burden you carry. Choose forgiveness, and trust the Wounded Healer to mend your aching heart.

Reflection

- Have you been holding on to an offense in your marriage?
- Do you freely forgive your husband? Or are you a slow or resistant forgiver?

Application

As you begin wrestling with what God is asking you to forgive, start by looking up these verses: Matthew 6:15; 18:21–22; and 1 John 1:9. Then write out the verses, personalizing them wherever possible. For example, this is how it might look for me: "But if you, *Lisa*, do not forgive others their trespasses, neither will your Father forgive your trespasses" (Matt. 6:15). *Ouch*. That's convicting!

Next, you might find it helpful to take out a separate piece of paper and write out the offense(s) you're struggling to forgive. And, if you're ready to grant forgiveness, take that paper and tear it up or throw it in a fire as a visible symbol of the step you're taking. Afterward, go to your husband and let him know you've forgiven him, and then enjoy the blessing of full reconciliation.

Prayer

Dear Heavenly Father, I am nearly overwhelmed when I consider how You have forgiven me and at such a cost. And although I know I shouldn't hold back from forgiving others in their turn, especially if they've humbly asked, I'm struggling to let it go. Help me to freely forgive as I've been forgiven and to trust You to heal my hurting heart. In Jesus's name, amen.

18

Anxiety

Do not be anxious about anything, but in everything by prayer and supplication with thanksgiving let your requests be made known to God.

Philippians 4:6

My poor husband. Last night, I suddenly awoke at 2:17 a.m. with a loud gasp. I sat straight up with a hand clutched to my racing heart, taking all the bedcovers with me. Without a clue as to what was happening, Matt lunged out of bed in full protect-the-family mode, ready to stop evil intruders or slay dragons or whatever it is that goes through a man's mind at two in the morning. I could feel his adrenaline surge from six feet away.

Oh dear, I felt so bad about the false alarm. Because we weren't dealing with dangerous intruders or fire-breathing dragons, only that horrible monster called *anxiety*. And, unfortunately, it wasn't the first time that week either.

The strange thing is that, while this might be familiar territory for you, I've never been an overly anxious person. Maybe it's my upbringing or my personality, but I've generally tended to take things in stride. But much has changed over the last few years, and I'm finding it increasingly difficult to shrug off worries or shake my apprehensions. It's not uncommon now for me to wake up like I did that night, with a weight bearing down so heavily on my heart that I feel I can hardly breathe.

This experience has given me new empathy for my friends who fight anxiety—perhaps friends like you. Women who walk around with a big knot in the middle of their chest. Sisters who find it hard to sleep, no matter what techniques or supplements they might try. Friends who struggle with a feeling strikingly similar to panic. We might have our own reasons for what makes us anxious, but our suffering is much the same.

If this is something you struggle with, then you're aware of how it takes a toll on your mind, your health, your home, and your marriage. And it's that last one I specifically want to address because, as you know, anxiety has an awful way of stealing the joy and peace from your relationship with your husband.

And I'm not talking only about red-alert alarming your husband in the middle of the night but also about how paralyzing anxiety can be for you. It's difficult to laugh, kiss, love (or sleep!) when you're consumed with anxious thoughts. Your distress doesn't affect only you; it can't help but impact him as well.

So let's take a look at what God says about anxiety: He tells us straight out that we are not to be anxious about *anything* (Phil. 4:6). Notice that He doesn't say we should worry only about the big things or real concerns (as opposed to all the other imagined ones we fret over that never come to pass), but *not one thing*.

Now, how is it possible not to worry about *anything*? Fair question. The encouraging answer is found in the following phrase: You pray and seek God for *everything* weighing on your heart and mind. There is nothing too big or too small to bring before our Almighty God. Therefore, bring *all things* before Him.

But the verse doesn't stop there. If you're looking for a small secret to a peaceful heart, you might well find it tucked into the last part of this verse, where we're told to come to God "with thanksgiving." Because, when your heart is overflowing with gratitude, it naturally flushes that ugly anxiety right out of there. Thankfulness and anxiousness cannot both share the same space: One of them has to go.

Last, I would encourage you to be open with your husband about your struggle with anxiety. If he's a believer, ask him if he'll pray for you. So many times, I've awakened my husband in the night (on purpose then) and asked him to pray over me. His intercession has helped calm my heart and draw us closer as a small way for us to walk through my anxious struggles together.

So *pray*, *seek*, *ask*, and *give thanks*. We serve an all-powerful God, and you can entrust all your fears and anxieties to His loving care.

Reflection

- Do you struggle with anxiety? Has it always been this way, or can you pinpoint when it started?
- What are some of the things that trigger your anxious thoughts?

Application

Begin by praying with thanksgiving. Keep it simple: *Dear Lord, I am worried about our finances but I want to trust in Your provision. Thank You for the food on our table today.* Or *Heavenly Father, I'm deeply concerned about my husband (or kids), but I know You love them even more than I do. Thank You for my marriage (or family) and the work You've done so far (get specific here).* These are only a couple of the many ways you can pray and supplicate with a thankful heart.

Prayer

Almighty God, I give my anxious thoughts to You. While there is much to worry about in this world, I know that You are wise and powerful, and I can count on You to care for me and the things that concern me. In Jesus's name, amen.

Note: If you struggle with more than the occasional bout of anxiety, I encourage you to seek help from a biblical counselor or medical professional.

19

Service

For you were called to be free, brothers and sisters; only don't use this freedom as an opportunity for the flesh, but serve one another through love.

Galatians 5:13 CSB

"That kind sir." That's what my mother-in-law called Matt's dad those last few years of her life. By then, he was a total stranger to her rather than her husband of over sixty years. So one day, I was feeling sorry for him and asked how he felt about his wife calling him "kind sir" instead of "honey" or "dear" or by his first name, Don.

He said, "Could be worse, I figure," and he shrugged and laughed. But the tears in his eyes told another story.

I don't know exactly when we first understood that Mom had developed Alzheimer's. It came on so gradually that it's difficult to pinpoint when we realized she had more than merely a forgetfulness problem; she suffered from something far more severe.

However, that day did come, and soon we were obligated to take the car keys from her for her own good. Before long, it was not safe for her to bake or cook. And toward the end, it became too difficult for her to dress or even feed herself. With hearts aching, we watched her slowly change from a strong, independent pioneer woman into a lost and helpless child.

But, just as slowly, Dad started taking over those everyday tasks for her. He'd lay out her outfits for the following morning and help her when she got tangled up in the sleeves. He'd prepare her oatmeal for breakfast and cook their supper every night. He'd cut up her food and go so far as to spoon it into her mouth when necessary. He'd carefully spot-clean her blouse where she'd spilled.

Dad was at her service from the time she woke up until at last he got her tucked into bed at night. *That kind sir.* He didn't complain, although sometimes, very rarely, I'd catch him quietly crying in his chair after she was safely sleeping. Then he'd look up and wipe his eyes with his ever-present handkerchief and apologize.

"Oh Dad" was all I could choke out. "What are you saying sorry for?"

And his dedication reminded me of what Jesus said about anyone who wanted to be great in God's kingdom and how they must first be *a servant* (Matt. 20:26). If that's the case, then my father-in-law was, in my view, a truly great man.

The puzzling part of this story is that here I was watching all of this sacrificial devotion in real time, genuinely moved and yet still somehow struggling to serve my husband in my own home. *Why doesn't he pick up those things? Why can't he take care of that? Why is this left for me to follow up on?* I admired my father-in-law's laying down of his life—and then resented my own opportunities to do the same.

So, maybe you struggle to serve too. You've asked yourself similar questions, possibly posed them to your husband. "*Why? Do I look like a servant to you?*"

That's an excellent question. *Do* you look like a servant? Because while it might not be a popular concept in today's culture, it's a very popular one in the kingdom of God. As Christ followers, we're called to serve—and not only to get the job done but to carry it out with a good attitude. "Rendering service *with a good will* as to the Lord and not to man" (Eph. 6:7).

In other words, when my father-in-law was busy washing Mom's dishes and doing her laundry, he wasn't only serving his wife; he was serving the Lord. Or when my husband was mopping our floors before I hosted a bridal shower yesterday (true story), then, yes, he was serving me but also the Lord.

And when you and I cheerfully *pick up those things, take care of this,* and *follow up on that,* then we, too, are "rendering service as to the Lord." A comforting thought, really. So with that in mind, consider how God may be calling you to be more servant-hearted toward Him—and your husband.

Reflection

- Do you embrace the idea of servanthood? Or is it something you chafe against?
- What are some of the ways you already serve your husband? Are there any other ways you could add that would bless your marriage?

Application

I have a good friend who's been married for thirty-six years, and she said the secret to their happiness is how they strive to out-serve one another. She laughed and made it sound like it was some kind of competition. Boy, do I love that idea! While not everyone is married to a spouse who wants to compete in service, it's still a worthy goal in a healthy Christian marriage.

If you're in a place where you'd like to find additional ways to serve in your marriage, consider what acts of service might mean the most to your husband. You might want to ask him outright what would bless him!

Prayer

Dear Heavenly Father, I recognize that even Your Son "came not to be served but to serve" (Matt. 20:28), and I desire to follow His example of sacrificial love. Show me how I can serve my husband better, and I pray that he would have a heart to serve me as well. In Jesus's name, amen.

20

Desire

I am my beloved's,
and his desire is for me.
Song of Solomon 7:10

I don't know if every newly married couple makes a "plan" for after the wedding ceremony, but Matt and I had one. We'd decided ahead of time that we would experience our first night together after we settled into a rustic resort, which meant a three-hour drive over to the other side of the mountain pass.

However, before heading to our honeymoon spot, we swung by his suburban apartment to pick up our two suitcases for the trip. And, as you might've already guessed, the original plan changed, and we did *not* wait until we reached the mountain resort.

Well, not exactly "we" because, to be more precise and much to my new husband's surprise, it was *me* who changed my mind—and his. I had no wish to wait another minute. As the Song of Solomon puts it: *My desire was for him.*

At that point in our lives together, I naïvely imagined that it would always be like this. That we'd always long for each other's bodies and look forward to the joys of intimacy—never slowing down until we were old and gray.

It's okay if you laugh. I don't mind. Especially if you've been married for any length of time. How could I have known at twenty-six what it might be like at thirty-six (with five children) or forty-six (with eight) or, for that matter, going on fifty-six?

Actually, it was when I was in my late thirties, pregnant with our seventh child, that something switched for me. Although I loved being a mom, I felt like my body was tapped out and overly touched by too many little hands. So while I never meant for it to happen, between bearing those seven babies, I'd somewhat lost that physical desire for my husband.

Please understand, my husband put zero pressure on me. Quite the opposite, he was both considerate and patient. Yet as my disinterest stretched from weeks to months, I grew increasingly concerned about the situation. We were still friends—but barely lovers—and I desperately wanted this to change. Neither of us had ever viewed sex as a duty—more of a gift and a pleasure—but then my desires changed.

Now I longed for things like sleep, adult conversation, a clean kitchen floor, and a bowl of mint-chip ice cream all to myself. Sharing my body with him was nowhere at the top of the list. On most nights, it wasn't on the list *anywhere.*

So one day, as I sat my great-with-child body down on a grassy hill to watch our other children play, I reflected with regret on the physical intimacy we'd lost and began to pray. Sheepishly at first. Although I've made many different highly personal requests to God over the years, *this* was a first. "Lord, renew my desire for my husband," I whispered. "I want to *want* him again." A simple prayer but sincere; I meant it with all my heart. And, while God doesn't always answer our requests *when* or *in the way* we hope, He did answer this one, and soon afterward.

We women can have many different reasons why we struggle with desire—or lack of it—but one thing I learned that day on that grassy hill is that there is nothing we can't bring before the Lord.

Maybe you, too, find you've lost your desire for your spouse (or the other way around). If this is your situation, have you taken it to the Lord in prayer? Ask Him to renew your passion or show you what needs to change to bring back that spark that's been missing. While this may be merely a season for you, it might also be helpful to seek biblical counseling for healing or better understanding.

Before closing, I want to recognize that this can be a complicated and sensitive subject for many. I can't pretend to know or fully grasp your particular situation; I am merely sharing a part of my own personal journey with you. At the very least, my hope is that our conversation here will encourage you to pray, hope, and find further help if necessary.

Reflection

- How would you describe your season of life right now? Has it affected your physical desire for your husband? Or his for you?
- Have you been intentional in making your sex life a priority? Is there anything you can do or change to make it better?

Application

In addition to prayer, when Matt and I are out of sync, we've found honest conversation to be helpful. We will set aside a time, away from the kids and other interruptions, to talk about how we're feeling, what we're struggling with, and what each thinks it's going to take to get back on track. While not always a comfortable discussion (for me), it's worth the awkwardness of laying it all out there. This might be a good starting place for you and your husband as well.

Prayer

Dear Heavenly Father, I'm asking You to give me a desire for my husband—and him for me. I want us to enjoy a healthy sex life together, as far as it is possible. Please heal any wounds, reveal any hidden sin, and restore our physical love for one another. In Jesus's name, amen.

Note: Sex is not a solution for abusive or manipulative marriages. If your husband uses sex to manipulate or guilt you, please seek counseling and outside help.

21

Patience

With all humility and gentleness, with patience, bearing with one another in love.

Ephesians 4:2

"Mommy, why did you marry Daddy?" The girls often asked me this question when they were young. I'm not sure why they kept asking, as they already knew the answer after having heard my reply many times before. My response was usually some variation of "Because your daddy was the most exciting man I'd ever met."

And it's true; he was and still is.

We hadn't even finished our first "real" date when Matt invited me to join him and a few friends on an extended sailing trip around the islands off the Canadian coast. While I didn't accept his crazy invitation, it did sound rather fun . . .

Maybe I beamed at him and was all in back then, but this wouldn't always be my response to Matt's wild ideas and proposals. It turns out that the kinds of things that sound thrilling when you're single and relatively free feel entirely different when you're married and expecting your first child. Such as when he walked into the kitchen the second year into our marriage and enthusiastically announced, "Whaddya say we move to St. Petersburg?" As in St. Petersburg, *Russia*.

I listened in stunned silence while he enthusiastically listed all the wonderful reasons we should live there until he noticed the tears quietly trickling down my face.

You can picture this, can't you? Seven months pregnant, seated at our apartment's small kitchen table, trying to imagine myself moving from Oregon to Russia. We might as well have been traveling to a different planet as far as I was concerned.

In my head, I was already packing up boxes, deciding what to bring and what to leave behind, all while wondering where exactly our baby would be born. I was mentally and emotionally exhausted before we ever stood up from the table. It didn't matter much that we didn't move to Russia that year (or any other year, so far); I'd traveled there and back in my mind. And what had been formerly thrilling about my husband had since turned into a source of frustration, stress, and sometimes tears.

If you happen to be married to a visionary, a dreamer, or the entrepreneur type, my guess is that you're right there with me. Or maybe you're sitting there thinking, "I only *wish* my husband would come up with an outside-the-box idea!" Perhaps you were drawn to your man for his stability that made you feel safe and secure—and now this same steadiness annoys you.

Who could've guessed that a husband would so test a woman's patience?

And yet love is *patient* (1 Cor. 13:4). Or—I like how it's put in the King James Version—it is *longsuffering*, which is the ability (or should I say the determination?) to *suffer long*. To endure an extended time without seeing change or achieving your desired outcome. This is a sacrificial willingness to "suffer" out of love for the other person.

Now, if you're a mother of young children, then you know how (little) people can try your patience. It seems they rarely do *what* you want them to do, much less *when* and *how* you want them to do it. So you're left to look up to the heavens and pray for patience while you wait for them to eventually get where you want them to be.

Marriage can be a bit like that. Maybe your husband is moving too fast with too many ideas, or perhaps he's poking along and seemingly stuck in a rut. He's too intense or too laid-back. Perhaps he's not stepping up, responding to your requests, or making the changes you desire. Whichever it is, the basic problem is that he's not where *you* want him to be.

So you find yourself losing patience.

Friend, everyone and every situation is different, but here's what I can say from my own experience of thirty years of marriage: People do grow, and changes do happen. And then I'll gently add, sometimes the person changing happens to be *you*. Over time, as you walk with the Lord, you will hopefully find that you are less easily irritated by the things your husband says or does. You might start to see those things that had seemed almost wrong as merely *differences*, and they might even become endearing if you let them.

So, if you find yourself frustrated or discouraged with your spouse, quickly remind yourself, *love is patient*. Embrace the longsuffering nature of love.

Reflection

- Do you find yourself more patient with friends or family than you are with your husband?

- If so, have you considered what makes you short with him when you extend grace to others around you? Why do you think that might be?

Application

You'll find numerous places in the Bible where we are instructed to practice patience. If this is an area you struggle with, you might want to write out one or more of these verses: Romans 8:25; 12:12; Galatians 6:9; Ephesians 4:2.

Next, identify something your husband says or does that frequently tries your patience. Then pray and ask God to show you how (and give you the strength!) to practice longsuffering in your situation.

Prayer

Dear Lord, help me have more patience with my husband. I want to be longsuffering, especially when it comes to his personality, his quirks, and even his shortcomings. I realize he has plenty of opportunity to be patient with me, so give me the grace to offer the same for him. In Jesus's name, amen.

22

Tenderhearted

Be kind to one another, tenderhearted, forgiving one another, as God in Christ forgave you.

Ephesians 4:32

It's not often that we get to see our oldest son—or, at least, not as often as we would like. Since Britain (his name, not the place) lives clear across the country from us, we only get to spend time together over the Christmas holidays and for our much-anticipated summer family vacation. A few short and cherished weeks a year.

So you can understand why we have a hard time sharing him when he's home. We're rather inclined to keep him to ourselves—with the only exception being our church gathering on Sunday—and to be candid, even then, I selfishly struggle a bit.

But I wasn't sorry we decided to attend church together during his last visit here. Otherwise, I would have missed out on seeing a side to my son that not everyone gets to see, one that deeply touches me.

One of the dear families in our home church recently adopted a beautiful little girl from India who has special needs (not unlike our own Avonléa's), and it was Britain's first time meeting her. Toward the end of the service, the child grew fidgety and fussy, and her mom found it increasingly difficult to keep her happy.

Britain leaned over to her and asked if he could try to help. I watched as he gathered up the tiny child into his strong arms and held her softly, securely there until, at last, she lay her head on his shoulder and fell fast asleep.

I still have a picture of that precious moment on my phone. Muscular young man and peacefully sleeping child. And I'll never forget how gentle he was with her—how careful of her fragile limbs and mindful of her rough start in life. How *tenderly* he treated her.

How I want to be that tenderhearted toward others—don't you?

We probably don't find tenderness too difficult when it comes to our children. Mothers' hearts naturally tend to soften when our kids are hurting or struggling, sympathizing if it's been a long day or they didn't get enough sleep. We console them when they're dealing with a personal disappointment, heartache, or trial. And we can usually see past their bad attitudes or out-of-proportion meltdowns, feeling genuine pity for their little hearts.

It can be a different story, though, when we're dealing with a grown man, especially the one we're married to. If he's had a hard day or is weighed down with pressures, we're not nearly as prepared to cut him slack or offer the same sympathy. "He's an adult," we tell ourselves. "He should know better." And why can't he *pull it together* in his circumstance or situation?

Yet, in Ephesians, God tells us to be "tenderhearted," right between "be kind to one another" and "forgiving one another"

(4:32). We're familiar with that first instruction and have surely encountered the third one, but what about that middle part about having a tender heart toward each other? As in, toward that grown man next to you?

The same word (*eusplanchnos*) translated as "tenderhearted" in Ephesians 4:32 is used again in 1 Peter 3:8: "Finally, be ye all of one mind, having compassion one of another, love as brethren, be pitiful [same *eusplanchnos*], be courteous" (KJV). I appreciate how the King James Version puts it here: "be pitiful." That is, *take pity*, my friends.

Maybe your thoughts leap to all the reasons why your husband doesn't merit such tenderness. A list of excuses is running through your mind right now. Yes, *why*? Why show sympathy to someone who doesn't particularly deserve it?

We find our answer in the last phrase of Ephesians 4:32: "as God in Christ forgave you." Our Heavenly Father has shown such undeserved kindness, such compelling tenderness toward us. Therefore, how can we not in turn extend this kind of heart toward others and in our marriage?

Although you weren't able to join us on the heartwarming Sunday morning when our son so tenderly cared for that sweet child, I hope the picture stirs your heart as much as it did mine. Oh, that we could be tenderhearted like that!

- What do you picture when you hear the word *tenderhearted*?
- How could you show more tenderness in your marriage?

Application

If you find it challenging to be tenderhearted toward your husband, consider why that might be. What holds you back or prevents you from showing tenderness? Then consider *why* God tells us to be tenderhearted toward one another. Why is it listed along with "brotherly love" and "a humble mind" (1 Pet. 3:8)? Write down as many reasons as you can why tenderness is included as one of the essentials in a Christian relationship.

Last, decide how you might demonstrate tenderness in your marriage. Would it be how you look at your husband? How you touch him? How you respond to him when he's feeling low or having a rough week? Write down two or three specific ways you can express a tender heart toward him.

Prayer

Dear Lord, help me to be more tenderhearted toward my husband. I want to treat him kindly, remembering the great kindness You've shown me. Give me a soft, compassionate heart for him. In Jesus's name, amen.

23

Sacrifice

Greater love has no one than this, than to lay down one's life for his friends.

John 15:13 NKJV

I had no idea when we first got married that I'd find myself waking up alone. And not only for a morning or two, but day after day for nearly five years. Every morning I opened my eyes and sleepily reached a toe over in search of his warm body, only to find a cold empty space where my husband had been hours before. I never did get used to not feeling his warmth next to me—each time marking the loneliest moment of my day.

And if you're wondering where my husband might have been so early in the morning and why I'd let this situation continue for so long, it's because Matt would be next door making coffee for his dad and getting him going on his day. Preparing his breakfast, helping him shuffle to the bathroom, and tucking him back into his favorite chair. After that, the routine generally included the two men watching and discussing the news, with Dad making his best attempts to solve the world's problems from his sage-green recliner across the room. But that's about as far as it went since he never again left the house after losing his wife and being placed on hospice care.

By then, Dad had lots of the loneliest moments in his life. Sharing a pot of coffee and the morning news with his youngest son was one of the few bright spots in his day.

Such a long, sweet string of sacrifice over those years. At first, Dad laying down his life for his confused and often forgetful wife. Then Matt giving up those morning hours—and so many more—for his dying dad. And me, making the smallest sacrifice of all, enduring some cold, lonely moments waking up without my man.

For better, for worse. For richer, for poorer. In sickness and in health. Even if you didn't include those familiar phrases in your wedding vows, I'm sure you have a sense of the sacrificial love called for in a Christian marriage. We recognize that no matter what life throws at us—loss, disappointment, injury, illness—as a couple, we're pledged to walk through the hardships together.

However, what sounds beautiful when you're dressed in a white bridal gown can seem less lovely when the time actually comes to live it out. Sacrificial love can be messy and often goes unseen and unrecognized. This kind of love might require preparing meals, losing sleep, wiping up bodily fluids, or surrendering personal dreams. Or maybe just waking up alone. Whatever it is, we rarely get to *choose* our sacrifice.

Perhaps that's where you're at right now. And it's definitely *not* a situation you would've chosen if it had been left up to you. Maybe you're laying down the smaller things, such as restful nights or financial security. But maybe you're making bigger sacrifices by forgoing freedoms, overlooking offenses, or giving up your need to be right. And what can make it more challenging is that no one appears to notice the very real cost of your loving sacrifice.

Oh friend, sacrificial love *is* costly. I don't know how it can ever be anything but painful to lay down your life for another.

And yet, you are *not alone*—however those loneliest moments might make you feel. You have a wonderful Savior who not only *sees* your sacrifice but also cares about the cost.

What's more, He has gone before you. The Bible tells us that Jesus Christ has "loved us and given Himself for us, an offering and a sacrifice to God" (Eph. 5:2 NKJV). He paid the ultimate price—gave up His very life—for you and me, to set us free from sin and shame. He gave up *everything* to reconcile us to our Heavenly Father, conquering death that we might live forever with Him in heaven.

And it's because of what Christ did for us that we can bear to walk in such love. This *costly, extravagant love.*

Reflection

- What have you been willing to sacrifice for your husband?
- In what ways do you think God might be asking you to "lay down your life" in your marriage?

Application

At times, we can secretly (or not-so-secretly) resent what we've been asked to sacrifice for our marriage. If this is you, then prayerfully ask the Lord how He can help you turn your bitterness into joy. Perhaps spend time reflecting on His ultimate sacrifice, how He went willingly, even joyfully, to the cross in His love for you (Heb. 12:2).

If you've been holding back on what you believe God is asking you to sacrifice for your marriage, why not take a step of obedience and lay it down before Him? Don't be worried if it's messy, unseen, or thankless. Remember that you are not alone and He knows the cost.

Prayer

Dear Heavenly Father, I am so grateful that You sent Your only Son to give His life to set me free from sin and shame. I want to follow His example and lay down my life in my marriage. Please reveal how I can best offer a deep, healthy, and sacrificial love for my husband. In Jesus's name, amen.

24

Contentment

Not that I am speaking of being in need, for I have learned in whatever situation I am to be content.

Philippians 4:11

Clearly, my friend was bothered by something. I watched as she moved through her newly remodeled kitchen with a heavy sigh and a disgruntled look on her face. Then, almost afraid to ask, I gently ventured, "Is something amiss, friend? You look upset."

Although she replied, "It's nothing; I'm fine," her body language told me a different story. She was anything but fine.

Since we'd known each other for many years, I felt I could press a bit further. So I asked her about a few possibilities that came to mind: "Did you and your husband get into an argument? Is somebody ill or injured?"

"No," she said. "It isn't anything like that."

But after a brief pause, she came out with it. The truth was, she was tired of living without a KitchenAid mixer. *And, honestly, all her friends had one—every single one of them!*

She was serious. And, sadly, this was not unusual coming from her. When I thought back over the time I'd known her, I realized that she often had some complaint or another about her husband and home. Their house needed repairs, her stuff was old or outdated—and her husband? She wondered whether he even cared.

Now the truth was, my friend lived in a gorgeous home, and her husband was known for being a really nice guy. He worked long hours and wasn't the most demonstrative man I'd ever met, but you couldn't doubt his love and faithfulness to his wife. From where I stood, the poor guy was earnestly doing his best—the recent kitchen remodel being one of many such attempts to make her happy.

But whatever it was, it was never *enough*.

My heart ached for both my friend and her husband, and I think yours would too. Here this woman had so much good in her life and yet she didn't have eyes to see it. Instead, she was miserable living in this unhappy prison that she'd made with her own hands.

As for her husband, I felt bad for him too. Try as he might, there was nothing right he could do for his wife. It wouldn't have mattered if he'd bought a bigger house, installed trendy bathroom tile, or replaced the current carpet, nothing—not even a commercial KitchenAid mixer—would have gone very far in solving their problems. Unfortunately, new stuff is never a lasting cure for discontentment.

In reality, my friend had everything she needed—maybe not everything she *wanted*, but certainly everything she needed (and, it could be argued, *more* than what most people have). What a tragedy!

So, how about you, friend? Do you find yourself always wanting more? In 1 Timothy 6:6, we're told there is "great gain" when contentment is added to godliness. So, if we want to enjoy riches or a happy, satisfying marriage, we can start by practicing the art of contentment.

For most of us, this begins with counting our blessings. First, try looking at the good gifts everywhere around you. Then, as that old familiar hymn says, *name them one by one*. For example, if you don't have the latest KitchenAid mixer, but you have a kitchen, that's a blessing! Or if your husband isn't as expressive as you'd like, but he has a steady job and comes home to you, tell him you're grateful!

Sometimes, we can convince ourselves that nothing will ever change or improve if we don't complain or register our dissatisfaction. This outlook is a deception that can rob us of our current joy. Choosing contentment doesn't mean you never mention something that would make your life easier or your heart fuller. We should feel free to communicate both our needs and our wants, and our husbands should listen carefully to our wishes. But the difference is that, rather than coming from a place of continual discontent, we're coming from a peaceful place of gratitude.

So, sister, let's count our many blessings and enjoy the wealth of riches that come with a contented life.

And my God will supply every need of yours according to his riches in glory in Christ Jesus. (Phil. 4:19)

Reflection

- Do you struggle with discontentment? Do you find yourself frequently wishing you had more, better, different?
- Or would you say you're generally satisfied with your life, your home, your husband?

Application

Take some time this week to reflect on your level of contentment. Consider asking your husband or a close friend if they'd describe you as content or discontent. If you find you struggle with a never-enough attitude, confess this to God and then to your husband. Tell your husband you want to change this, for your own sake as much as his.

Prayer

Dear Heavenly Father, Your Word says that "godliness with contentment is great gain" (1 Tim. 6:6), and I desire this kind of gain. I want a rich life full of joy and thankfulness. Please open my eyes to Your goodness everywhere around me and help me exude my gratefulness to others, especially my husband. In Jesus's name, amen.

25

Trials

The Lord is near to the brokenhearted
and saves the crushed in spirit.
Psalm 34:18

Our fourth son was born with beautiful blue eyes and the sweetest temperament. He was our last child, the youngest of eight, so it was only natural for our entire family to dote on him. And everything was just as it should have been, at least at first. He smiled, cooed happily, waved his arms, and kicked his tiny feet. This little one never gave me a moment's concern.

Until one Sunday when everything changed.

A friend and I were standing at the back of the church, both of us holding our babies, who were born only a few weeks apart. I was watching as her daughter grabbed the teething toy her mama was holding out when it suddenly dawned on me: Our baby boy didn't grab like that. He didn't reach for toys or grasp for things at all. Come to think of it, he had been slower and slower in reaching several milestones typical for a baby his age.

Now, why would that be? Up until then, I'd chalked it up to an easygoing temperament, but on that Sunday morning, I came to realize it might be something far more serious.

As a test, I quietly held a stuffed animal in front of our son's face to see what he would do. He didn't reach for the little bear; he never even blinked. Instead, he stared blankly without seeing the toy held merely inches from his eyes.

There was a reason our baby boy didn't reach for food or toys: *He was blind.*

And the news was beyond devastating to us. *Wasn't it enough that we already had one child with severe special needs? Was there some test we hadn't passed that required us to face another? How could God allow another shattering blow?* We wept, mourned, and poured out our grieving hearts to God.

Although Matt and I both shared this sorrow, we did not mourn in the same way or for the exact same reasons. Matt worried about our son's future, while I worried more about what he needed now. Matt took each tragedy separately, while to me they were closely connected. Matt didn't necessarily feel responsible for what had happened, while I couldn't help wondering, as the mother, if it was something I had or hadn't done. Both of us were heartbroken—but each walked this trial in a different way.

Have you known such heartbreak in your life? Maybe not with a baby born blind, but with some other disappointment or undoing? Perhaps you've experienced a family tragedy or a fractured friendship. Possibly something terribly painful in your marriage.

And maybe your husband shares your grief, or maybe you feel as though you're on your own.

If it's the first, you'll have to accept that he might well view and process the situation differently than you do. Give him grace to walk through it in his own way, and ask the same of him. Take turns with your tears, or cry out to God together where you can.

If it's the second, and you feel quite alone in your sorrow, I want to say that my heart goes out to you. Although I can't answer your *Why me?* or *Why this?* any more than I could my own, here's one thing I can tell you: The Lord promises He is near to the brokenhearted. He is close by, and He cares for your shattered heart. We may never understand the reasons or get all the answers to our questions, but He is with us in our deepest heartache.

> When you pass through the waters, I will be with you;
> and through the rivers, they shall not overwhelm
> you;
> when you walk through fire you shall not be burned,
> and the flame shall not consume you. (Isa. 43:2)

In your darkest, saddest moments, you can count on God to lovingly stay by your side. In time, He will heal your heart and bind your wounds (Ps. 147:3). No matter what trial you're walking through, sweet friend, know that you can trust Him with your broken heart.

Reflection

- Have you walked through a trial with your husband? Do you feel like that experience drew you closer together, or did you feel rather alone?
- Do you know that you can trust God with your greatest trials?

Application

If you've never kept a journal, you might find it helpful to start one. Writing down your story on paper—recording the details, describing your emotions, asking the questions—can be both healing and restorative. And there's no need to be eloquent or to choose your words carefully; simply pour out your heart to your Heavenly Father, who cares for you.

You might also consider reading through the book of Psalms—one short verse, passage, or psalm each day. Maybe get out a Bible highlighter and mark those places that directly speak to your soul. You'll find that the entire book is full of cries to God, interspersed with rejoicing and remembering His goodness and faithfulness. The Psalms have brought much comfort to me in my times of trial, and I pray the same for you.

Prayer

Dear Heavenly Father, You know better than anyone the difficulty and disappointment I'm facing. Hear my cries, and help me believe You're near. Comfort and heal my broken heart, I pray. In Jesus's name, amen.

26

Miracles

You are the God who works wonders;
you have made known your might among the
peoples.

Psalm 77:14

I can't say I acted in faith. In truth, it was more out of numb obedience that I agreed for our church family to pray over our baby a month after learning of his blindness. Privately, I found it to be a painful process, knowing full well that our baby would never see—a fact confirmed by at least two doctors. Maybe everyone else could afford to hope for healing, but I could not; it hurt too much.

And yet we agreed for the elders of our church to anoint our son with oil and pray over him, just like Scripture instructs (James 5:14). Matt gently placed our baby on a soft blanket in the middle of the living room while many gathered around him to pray. But not me; I kept my distance, my eyes wide open to watch my child—and my spirit closed to what God could do.

That's how it happened that I was the first to see the shaft of light break through the otherwise cloudy day and shine through the skylight directly down on our baby boy. I don't remember gasping, though perhaps I did because soon everyone was staring at our son basking in the brightest light you can imagine. Let's put it this way: If you were ever going to make up a miracle, this is just how it would appear.

After a long hush, someone closed us with a somber *amen*, and I quickly gathered our baby back in the comfort of my arms.

Following the service, several people offered their unhelpful, overly optimistic observations. "I think his eyes look a little different now, don't you?" Or "Ooh! I believe I caught some eye contact just then!" And so on. I smiled outwardly, but inwardly, each comment was like a small stab to this mama's heart. Oh yes, why shouldn't they have hope? They didn't have anything to lose.

Yet, before the day was out, even I had to admit that something had changed. Our baby had this new bright-eyed look, almost as if he was seeing the world for the very first time. Then he looked right at me and *smiled*—not because I'd made any noise but as though he recognized me, as though he *saw* me, his mother.

Finally, because we couldn't wait a minute longer, Matt and I performed the old, now-familiar toy test on him. We silently held up a plush toy in front of his face and—can you believe it?—he *reached* for it.

A genuine miracle.

As I write this, I wonder if you're in a place where you're desperately longing for a miracle. Maybe something to do with your children, your health, or your financial situation. Or perhaps it's your marriage that needs the miracle. And maybe you find it hurts far too much to hope.

I can hear that. But I also believe in miracles. I should; I've watched one happen. So I'm ready to hold out hope for *your* miracle—even with the understanding that God doesn't always answer with the miracle we're wanting. It's true that our son, who was blind, can now see; it's also true that our daughter, who had a stroke before birth, cannot walk and likely never will (barring another miracle!). We are comforted in the confidence that, truly, "all things work together for good to those who love God, to those who are the called according to His purpose" (Rom. 8:28 NKJV). He is always good—miracle granted or not.

Moreover, I've witnessed more than that one miracle. I've seen friends on the brink of divorce, papers waiting to be signed, who have reconciled and repaired their marriage. Others who have made grave mistakes or walked in sin, who have since repented and restored their relationship. These were undoubtedly answers to prayer. But I'd take it further: Each of these breakthroughs was every bit as much a miracle as healing a baby boy from blindness.

So, friend, and I say this with much compassion, let's pray in faith. Hope for our miracle. And trust God to carry us through whatever tomorrow holds.

Reflection

- Are you in a place where you're hoping for a miracle? Looking for a much-needed answer to prayer?
- Do you believe God works all things together for good? Do you trust that He sees you and is at work in your marriage?

Application

For just a moment, set aside that situation or relationship that feels so impossible right now and consider the following verses on the power of prayer:

- "Therefore I tell you, whatever you ask in prayer, believe that you have received it, and it will be yours" (Mark 11:24).
- "And my God will supply every need of yours according to his riches in glory in Christ Jesus" (Phil. 4:19).

Now, with a renewed sense of God's response to our prayers, commit your "impossible" situation to Him. You might also want to write down the names of a few trusted friends, family members, or ministry leaders whom you can ask to join you in your prayers.

Prayer

Dear Lord, I am facing a seemingly impossible situation in a relationship that feels hopeless, but I'm choosing to trust You to make a way. If it's Your will, I pray that You will perform a miracle here. In Jesus's name, amen.

27

Kindness

Put on then, as God's chosen ones, holy and beloved, compassionate hearts, kindness, humility, meekness, and patience.

Colossians 3:12

You might have read my story elsewhere of how a complete stranger taught me an unforgettable lesson on kindness—a true story.[1] And although I only met this woman one time and it's unlikely she'll ever know it, God used her to greatly impact my marriage.

The short version is that this woman was a cashier at our local grocery store. She was evidently having a rough day and in turn taking it out on the rest of us who were standing in her line. I became annoyed by her slow pace and snarky attitude, mulling over what I wanted to say to her when the time came for me to purchase my groceries.

Yet when my turn finally arrived for this cashier to ring up my items, I had an unexpected change of heart. Rather than communicating the impatience I'd been feeling toward her, I felt a prompting by the Spirit to express kindness instead. So I smiled warmly and pretended not to notice her gruff manner. I asked her how her day was going (not so well, not surprisingly) and told her I hoped it would get better. Then I thanked her kindly for her help.

The effect was astonishing. The woman visibly cheered up and picked up the pace, even half-smiled as I left the store. Who would've thought there would be so much power in a kind word?

But the lesson wasn't over, because I had another opportunity when I got home from my many errands that day. As it happened, my husband was also having a rugged day and called to say it didn't look like he'd be able to keep our long-planned appointment.

And that call made me instantly furious. All the rushing around I'd done that afternoon was for nothing after he had *promised* to make it home in time. Once again, I was prepared to pour out my frustration on the other person—although this time the situation was more serious, it wasn't even the other person's fault, *and* the target was the man I'd married.

Then, for the second time that day, I suddenly experienced a clear moment of conviction. Only a few hours earlier, I'd decided to show kindness to a total stranger. Could I not now make the same choice for my husband?

I could, and somehow I did. Rather than communicating how much he'd let me down, I genuinely attempted to express sympathy instead. I told him I was sorry he'd had a difficult day and—not to worry—I'd reschedule our appointment for another time.

Complete silence.

My husband didn't say anything for several seconds as he processed this response from me. Here I had responded with kindness and sympathy when I typically would have reacted with irritation and anger—and his relief was palpable.

Choosing compassion that afternoon had more of an effect than I could have guessed—on both my husband *and* me. He was less defensive and more apologetic, and my heart was softer and calmer—all because of a bit of kindness.

So, can I ask you what might be a hard question? Do you find it easier to be kind to that grumpy cashier or that rude server at the restaurant than to your own husband? Because the Bible tells us as believers to *be kind to one another* (Eph. 4:32) and to *put on kindness* (Col. 3:12). We are to show kindness to *everyone*—be it a stranger, friend, or husband—much the way God graciously showers *us* with kindness.

So why not try it with the man you married? Be kind to him with the words you speak, the tone you use, and the actions you take. Decide you want to be a kind wife.

Reflection

- Can you think of ways you show kindness toward your husband?
- Do you speak kindly? Use a kind tone of voice?

Application

If you're convicted (as I was!) that you've not been as kind toward your husband as you should be, consider confessing it to him and asking his forgiveness. Then resolve to show more kindness—be as specific as possible about what that might look like—and start fresh tomorrow.

Here are some more verses on kindness to further inspire you:

- "Whoever pursues righteousness and kindness will find life, righteousness, and honor" (Prov. 21:21).
- "She opens her mouth with wisdom, and the teaching of kindness is on her tongue" (Prov. 31:26).
- "He has told you, O man, what is good; and what does the LORD require of you but to do justice, and to love kindness, and to walk humbly with your God?" (Mic. 6:8).
- "Love is patient and kind" (1 Cor. 13:4).

Prayer

Dear Lord, thank You for all the kindness You've so freely showered on me. I want to have the "law of kindness" on my tongue (Prov. 31:26 NKJV) and a spirit of kindness toward my husband. Help me be a kind wife. In Jesus's name, amen.

28

Anger

Be not quick in your spirit to become angry,
for anger lodges in the heart of fools.

Ecclesiastes 7:9

Just like you and Dad."

That's what one of our daughters said was the kind of marriage she desired. She wanted to laugh like we do, to snuggle and stay up late. Apparently, we made marriage look like a whole lot of fun.

She was only a little girl back then, and now that same girl is grown with a serious boyfriend of her own. So it feels more urgent to pack in everything I've ever wanted her to know about love and marriage. Okay, maybe not *everything*—but still, to be more transparent about the struggles that also come with marriage.

So I started the following conversation with something like this. "Hey, hon, you should know that someday your man is going to say or do something that's going to make you furious—and I mean M-A-D, mad."

Curious, she waited for me to continue.

"Although it might be hard to imagine right now, at some point, he *will* infuriate you. And when that happens, I want you to remember our talk today. Because if you're not prepared, it might throw you off. Possibly make you wonder if you're truly meant for each other."

I felt her lean in to me. For a brief moment, back to being my little girl again, but only for a moment.

Then this lovely young woman beside me asked, "But what if we were really, *really* determined to love each other? Like you and Dad. Then he wouldn't make me crazy-mad, would he?"

Maybe not. Maybe she'll be different from me, different from you. But I doubt it.

So many wives have confided in me how often they struggle with anger. Some of these are the quiet, stuffer types, and others are the bring-it-on types, but all of them have one thing in common: *anger.*

It would seem that you and I are not alone.

But wait, there's good news. We're not alone, *and* we're not helpless. Although I'm not a certified counselor, I do have a winning biblical strategy that I've shared with my daughter and can share with you too—especially for those situations when your husband has said or done something that pushes your buttons.

Know this, my beloved brothers [and sisters]: let every person be quick to hear, slow to speak, slow to anger; for the anger of [wo]man does not produce the righteousness of God. (James 1:19–20)

First, I recommend waiting to communicate with your husband until after you've cooled down. The Bible has a lot to say about being "slow to anger," and that's smart advice.

The next thing I'd advise is to pray about it. Prayer can both settle your soul and clarify your thinking. Pray for him, and pray for yourself.

Then, determine whether the issue is worth getting worked up over. It might be an offense you can overlook—or maybe not. And if *not*, be ready to identify the hurt or fault the best you can.

Next, approach him in love. And this means don't come after him with eyes blazing (see the first step). Come prepared to listen; be "quick to hear." He might have his own side to the story.

Finally, choose forgiveness. If you've sinned in your anger, then ask him to forgive you. If he is also at fault, then forgive him too—not necessarily because he deserves it or because it's easy but because you've been forgiven so much by our Savior.

After that, the two of you can start afresh—no longer crazy-mad but hopefully crazy in love again.

Reflection

- How well do you deal with your anger in your marriage?
- What steps have you taken to control your temper and deal with anger in a healthy way?

Application

I find it encouraging to see how much the Bible addresses the topic of anger, don't you? The sheer number of scriptural passages tells us that this is a common struggle and that there's something we can do about it.

This week, begin by observing the following verses: Psalm 37:8; Proverbs 14:29; 15:1; 19:11; and Ephesians 4:26. Not only the ones that say "refrain from anger," but also the one that says "be angry (and do not sin)." Write down the benefit to the person who is slow to anger; then, conversely, what happens when we're quick to lose our temper.

Perhaps you're in a season or situation where you need a strong visual reminder of what Scripture says about handling your anger. If so, then why not write out some of these verses and put them in strategic places throughout your home where you can readily look up and read them in an instant. You might even want to read them out loud!

Prayer

Dear Heavenly Father, I do not want to be an angry woman. Help me learn to control my temper and express my anger and concerns in a healthy, godly way. Calm my spirit, Lord, so I can be the wise wife I desire to be. In Jesus's name, amen.

Note: I want to reiterate that I am not a professional counselor; my qualifications are primarily as an older married Christian woman. And so, while I will encourage you to study these Scripture verses and take them to heart, if you (or your husband) have a serious issue with anger, I urge you to get help from a qualified biblical counselor.

29

Hope

But the LORD takes pleasure in those who fear him,
in those who hope in his steadfast love.

Psalm 147:11

W ell, those two will wake up hating each other," one of the guests confidently predicted as he took another bite of our wedding cake. He was an invited guest, as well as one of the pastors of the church we had formerly attended, so the statement was as surprising as you're probably picturing. Apparently, I had just pledged my life to someone whom I would grow to hate before I even got out of bed in the morning.

And that's not the only time I've heard doom spoken over our marriage.

The second time I learned that there was "no chance" for us was eight years later, after the birth of our fifth child, who was born with severe brain damage. The NICU head doctor pulled me into the hospital hallway to inform me, "Eighty-five percent of the marriages between parents of children like yours with severe special needs end in divorce." Otherwise stated, our marriage was statistically destined to dissolve.

Two people we had reason to respect and trust had little or no hope for a happy, lasting union for us.

I know. Who would speak such devastating words over a couple? Or you may not be surprised to hear it at all. Perhaps you've heard similar statements spoken over your own romance, such as "They'll never make it," or "They've got too much going against them," or "Those two had such a rough start, there's no fixing it now." And now you're starting to believe it.

Or maybe it's not other voices that have discouraged you but dark whispers of your own. You come from a family with a long history of divorce, and you wonder if it's only a matter of time before you end up there as well. Or you and your husband may have made so many mistakes or struggled with so many problems that you can't see a way forward.

It feels hopeless.

And perhaps it would be. Except for one important life-changing, life-giving truth: Our God is a Redeemer, and *nothing* is ever hopeless in Him. He is able to make a way where there doesn't seem to be one. He can heal wounds and reconcile relationships that no one thought possible.

While we could look at many verses on the power of God to break through barriers and overcome hurdles, let me share with you a couple of my favorite verses found in Ephesians.

> Now to him who is able to do far more abundantly than all that we ask or think, according to the power at work within us, to him be glory in the church and in Christ Jesus throughout all generations, forever and ever. Amen. (Eph. 3:20–21)

You can see why I love this passage, can't you? In particular, the part about God being able to do "far more abundantly"—or, in the King James Version, "exceedingly abundantly"—than anything we could ask or even think. And how can this be? It is because of His *dynamis* (in the Greek), or His power to perform miracles, and there is nothing too hard for Him.[1]

Yes, God is able—more than able.

So, if you're struggling with hopelessness in your marriage right now, put your hope in the God who redeems, remembering He wants to renew and restore your relationship even more than you do. My prayer is that you will abound in hope, friend.

> May the God of hope fill you with all joy and peace in believing, so that by the power of the Holy Spirit you may abound in hope. (Rom. 15:13)

Reflection

- Have you ever heard negative or discouraging words spoken over your marriage?
- Do you have hope for your marriage? And do you believe God is powerfully at work in you?

Application

If you are wrestling with discouraging voices—whether someone else's or your own—then determine right now that you will drown out those voices with the Voice of Truth. One way to do this is to write out as many true statements as you can based on the promises in God's Word. Here are a few examples that come to my mind:

- He will renew my strength as I wait on Him (see Isa. 40:31).
- With God, all things are possible (see Matt. 19:26).
- I hope for what I do not yet see (see Rom. 8:24–25).

And, if you want to keep going, here are some more encouraging verses for you: Psalm 39:7; Jeremiah 29:11; Romans 12:12; Colossians 1:27; Hebrews 11:1; and 1 Peter 1:3. I anticipate you'll be overflowing with hope by the time you're done with this study!

Prayer

Dear Heavenly Father, I pray that You will fill my heart with hope. Help me to believe that with You, all things are possible. In faith, I want to trust that You are working in ways that I cannot yet see. In Jesus's name, amen.

30

Honesty

Lying lips are an abomination to the LORD,
but those who deal truthfully are His delight.
Proverbs 12:22 NKJV

Surely, I can't be the only one who impulsively cut her own bangs as a young girl. But I can't imagine that every girl lied about it as I did.

At the time, Fran, a friend and neighbor who rather conveniently lived across the street from us, kindly offered to cut my hair. And so, every couple of months, I walked over to get my hair cut in her teal-green guest room turned temporary salon.

Fran noticed my handiwork right away. "What have you done to your hair? Did you cut it yourself?"

"No," I said. "I didn't."

"That's so strange! It looks like you cut it," she said, shaking her head. "You must have some pretty bad breakage going on."

But I only stared back at her with wide-eyed sincerity, letting her think that some strange phenomenon had swept over me, distinctly leaving the impression of badly chopped bangs. I'm so ashamed; I lied straight to her face. And she believed me (though goodness knows why!).

How many times I've recalled that encounter in Fran's guest room, wishing she would've called me out. Truly, I wish she had caught me in my lie and named it for what it was. Not that I blame Fran at all, but it was a pivotal moment where consequences rather than credulity would have served me better.

Because on that day, I learned that I could tell a lie and get away with it. And that there are situations where avoiding the truth could mean saving myself from embarrassment or awkwardness or more. Not that cutting my bangs turned me into a compulsive liar, but I'll admit that I tucked this experience away with a newfound awareness that a little lie could be my get-out-of-jail-free card when backed into a corner.

Or so I thought.

But you and I both know that there's nothing free about dishonesty. And while I didn't always tell a bald-faced lie as I did to dear Fran, I occasionally resorted to half-truths or dropped unpleasant details when it served me. Nevertheless, I felt comforted that I told the truth *most of the time.*

Until in came Matt Jacobson. Probably the most honest man I know. And after I married him, I became convicted and repented of my sinful habit of half-truths. He and I committed to being truthful in all our communications—telling each other everything without holding back or holding out. Together we pledged to live a life *without shadows.*

So, now that I've openly confessed my bad haircutting practices (and yes, I still cut my own bangs) and worse, my youthful lies, I want to talk about *honesty* and its place in marriage.

And if you're concerned, thinking *Oh, but I've hidden or denied things far worse than a bad haircut,* you're not the only one. I could say the same, as well as others here. Yet I can also testify that God is gracious to forgive and that my marriage is all the stronger for having repented, confessed, and gone all in on truth. This freedom is waiting for you as well.

The fact is, we live in a world where hidden or partial truth—a small deceit, a slight exaggeration, or the little white lie—is considered no big deal. No, it goes farther than that; the world promotes dishonesty as practical, unavoidable—necessary even—for self-preservation. So it can be no surprise that some of us might carry that ungodly perspective into our marriage.

The Bible holds an entirely different view of truth, however. As Christians we're straight-out instructed, "Do not lie to one another" (Col. 3:9), and in Proverbs we're told, "Lying lips are an abomination to the LORD" (12:22). The Word of God is clear that lying has no place in the life of a Christian—nor in a Christian marriage.

But that's not all Proverbs has to say. While the Lord detests "lying lips," the reverse is also true: "He delights in those who are trustworthy" (12:22). As believers, don't we want to delight the Lord more than anything? Then we must tell the truth, no matter what the cost, and live honestly.

So, friend, if you don't already, start enjoying the freedom and blessings that come with living a transparent, truth-filled life. No secrets. No lies. No shadows. Only the truth in love.

Reflection

- Do you practice complete honesty in your marriage?
- Are there any changes or confessions you need to make to enjoy a full-truth relationship?

Application

Spend a few moments searching your heart and seeking the Lord on the level of honesty in your marriage. Are there any situations where you've been less than honest? Where you've hidden or disguised something? If so, I encourage you to confess them to God and then to your husband. And don't let the Enemy, "the father of lies" (John 8:44), convince you that this step will only make it worse, because it's not true. Instead, you'll find that confession and a clean slate can bring renewed light and life into your relationship.

Prayer

Dear Heavenly Father, I know that "those who deal truthfully" (Prov. 12:22 NKJV) are Your delight, and that's what I desire. I want to walk in truth and enjoy the blessings of honest marriage communication. Help us both to be fully transparent and truthful with one another. In Jesus's name, amen.

31

Prayer

Praying at all times in the Spirit, with all prayer and supplication. To that end, keep alert with all perseverance, making supplication for all the saints.

Ephesians 6:18

People never change. That's what I've always heard and, up until that unusual Saturday morning, what I had always experienced. I'm not saying people never grow or mature, but to really *change*? Rarely.

So, after nearly five years of sharing our home with Matt's parents, and due to his mother's increasingly frustrating behavior, I told Matt I couldn't take it any longer. Despite having invited them to stay with us "until the end of their days," I was in a place where another week felt too burdensome for me, much less another year . . . or decade or two.

I'm sorry, but I just couldn't do it.

Matt had tried addressing my grievances with his mom after I had gotten nowhere with her. Even my father-in-law had spoken to her on my behalf—asking her to be kinder and more respectful—but to no avail. She was not one to budge and certainly not one to apologize. She was one strong, set-in-her-ways woman.

And I'd had enough. But before we took the drastic step of disinviting his parents, Matt asked if I would be willing to pray about it for another week.

Yet here's the thing: I *had* been praying about this painful situation and for my unmoving mother-in-law—going on five years now—and as far as I could tell, it hadn't made a bit of difference.

Still, I reluctantly agreed to pray for one more week.

Then *six days* later, early on a Friday morning, I knocked on Mom's door to borrow a cup of flour to make biscuits. However, when she opened the door, I was alarmed to see she had been weeping. My heart dropped, as I knew something truly awful must have happened since I'd never caught her crying before—not one time.

And that's when I heard the words I never thought I'd hear from her lips: "Oh Lisa, can you ever forgive me? I've been such a tyrant, and I don't know how you've put up with me all these years." She made those astonishing statements and then explained how she had been in the middle of her morning devotions when suddenly the Holy Spirit convicted her.

Just like that. An impossible answer to prayer.

Now, friend, if God can turn around my never-say-sorry mother-in-law, then I can tell you two things for sure: One, He does hear and answer our prayers. Two, He doesn't always need us to change someone else. Sometimes He does it without any help at all but by the Holy Spirit in response to our faithful prayers.

So, if you're in a place where you're beginning to wonder if God is listening to your prayers for your marriage, let me reassure you: He is listening, and He does care. Indeed, He doesn't always answer our requests *when* and exactly *how* we want them answered. At times it might feel slow in coming; other times, it's our heart or perspective that He changes, not the situation. But this you can count on: He is both sovereign and loving, and you can fully trust Him with your marriage. He perfectly loves you both.

> Be anxious for nothing, but in everything by prayer and supplication, with thanksgiving, let your requests be made known to God; and the peace of God, which surpasses all understanding, will guard your hearts and minds through Christ Jesus. (Phil. 4:6–7 NKJV)

Reflection

- Do you faithfully pray for your husband? For your relationship with each other?
- If there's a change you've been hoping to see, have you committed it to prayer?

Application

Consider the place of prayer in your daily life. While prayer can often be viewed as something we save for church or around the dinner table, in truth, God invites us to talk to Him about *everything* and at *any time*. He wants you to take your concerns, hopes, challenges, and victories before Him! You can entrust *all* aspects of your marriage to the hands of Him who cares for you.

Perhaps this is a good week for you to start a regular practice of prayer. Maybe you'll want to get up a little earlier in the morning or ask your husband if he'll pray with you before turning in for the night. Or you can develop the habit of praying as you drive in to work or on your way to pick up the kids. Maybe you'll decide to start a prayer journal and write down your requests—and answers!—in a notebook for this specific purpose.

Prayer

Dear Heavenly Father, I'm thankful I can come to You with all that's on my heart at any time. I want to make prayer an essential part of my day and night, trusting You with my life and marriage. Help me to have faith that You hear and answer my prayers. In Jesus's name, amen.

32

Purity

Let no one despise you for your youth, but set the believers
an example in speech, in conduct, in love, in faith, in purity.

1 Timothy 4:12

I was only thirteen when I met my first *real* boyfriend. I can still remember his name and where we went for our first "date." We walked over to the local bowling alley along with our two best friends, his and mine. And the fact that I despise bowling tells you that he must have been a pretty special eighth grader. But after a whirlwind romance that lasted a good ten to twelve days, we broke up for some trivial reason I can no longer recall.

Although that (very) young man might've been my first boyfriend, he wouldn't be the last. I had officially entered that wild, unpredictable world of boys and attraction and enticement. No turning back now. "Single and seeking" would be my story line for the next thirteen years.

However, let me stop here and recognize that unlike so many, I enjoyed the benefit of being brought up by loving parents and under solid church teaching—many people who offered a positive, healthy sense of purity. Even so, I struggled as a single.

I was suddenly filled with so many questions and confused by these newfound desires. *Besides saying no to sex, what did "walking in purity" really mean? What do you do with sexual desire while "waiting"? And when would this stupid battle ever end?* For most of these questions, I figured the answer was generally the same—get married.

But you and I know that marriage is not the magic solution to sexual purity.

Now, before we go much further in this conversation, let me clarify what we're *not* talking about—your husband. Obviously, he's an important part of the discussion; it's only that my husband, Matt, will be addressing the men, and you can count on him to speak plainly and powerfully to the guys on the topic of purity. (He also offers an excellent course on getting free and staying free from pornography and sexual sin.[1])

So, instead of discussing what your man might be wrestling with—although his wrestling would understandably affect you too—let's talk for now about the struggle that might be yours. Or, if not yours personally, perhaps that of a close friend or family member. Whatever the specific issue might be—whether it's viewing pornography, satisfying yourself sexually (masturbation), watching sensual movies or reading books thinly disguised as romance novels, or any other sexual temptation not listed here—one thing I do know is this: If you are a follower of Christ, you do not need to live in sin or under the weight of its shame. Such sexual sin does not need to, and *should not*, be part of your life in Him. You've been set free.

> We know that our old self was crucified with him in order that the body of sin might be brought to nothing, *so that we would*

no longer be enslaved to sin. For one who has died has been set free from sin. (Rom. 6:6–7)

Although Scripture teaches that we're no longer enslaved, many believers have bought the lie from the Enemy that we are stuck in our sin. *Hopelessly.* Satan wants you to believe that you are helpless, when you are anything but that—you are a child of God, indwelt by the Holy Spirit, and you have the power to say no to lustful desires (see Gal. 5:16).

So, if you've fallen or given in to temptation . . . yet again? Remember, our God is a Redeemer! He freely forgives when you repent from your sin, and He is more than able to restore. Knowing this, my friend, I encourage you to come forward, confess and repent, and then enjoy the beauty and blessing that come with walking in purity.

Reflection

- Do you struggle with sexual sin—in what you read, watch, think, or touch?
- Have you confessed this struggle or sin to God and your husband?

Application

If you struggle with sexual sin and haven't done so yet, start by confessing your sin to your Heavenly Father and then to your husband. As embarrassing or awkward as this conversation might feel, it's essential you come clean in your marriage. The Enemy will do his best to convince you this secret should remain in the dark, but this couldn't be farther from the truth. So bring sin out into the light and see what happens next! Watch how much of its ugly power fades right before your eyes with even this first simple step.

> Walk as children of light . . . and try to discern what is pleasing to the Lord. Take no part in the unfruitful works of darkness, but instead expose them. . . . But when anything is exposed by the light, it becomes visible, for anything that becomes visible is light. (Eph. 5:8–14)

Prayer

Dear Lord, I know my sexuality is a beautiful gift from You, and I want to enjoy what You've designed without suffering from sin or shame. I call on You as my Rock and Redeemer to ask that You restore what's been broken and break any chains that hold me. Help me to walk in the light and enjoy the freedom found in sexual purity. In Jesus's name, amen.

Note: If you've experienced sexual abuse or other similar trauma, then I highly recommend you seek out a professional biblical counselor for further help in your healing.

33

Goodness

But the fruit of the Spirit is love, joy, peace, patience, kindness, *goodness*, faithfulness, gentleness, self-control; against such things there is no law.

Galatians 5:22–23

"Why don't you two come live with us?"

Looking back, I'm amazed at how casually we threw out that invitation for Matt's parents to consider. It seemed reasonable enough in our season and, really, a natural solution for all of us. We had a houseful—with four kids ages five and under—so we could use the extra hands, and they were looking for a place to live. So, why not?

Yes, why not? And just like that, Matt's parents moved in and stayed with our family until the end of their years.

Although, when we made the offer, we had no idea what lay ahead for all of us. There was no way to anticipate that we'd end up caring for Mom as she took that long, painful journey with Alzheimer's. Or that immediately following Mom's passing, there would be several years of looking after Dad while he was placed on hospice care.

One right after the other—both of his dear parents. An extensive, exhausting, sad, and sometimes surprisingly sweet season. Yet once this challenging season had passed, rather than feeling the relief I'd expected, I felt strangely empty and aching. Hollowed out. And I found I couldn't move on and get back to living fully like before.

If at this point you're asking, "Now, what does all this sad stuff have to do with goodness?" it comes in soon, I promise, and we have my husband to thank for it.

"Hey, babe, look out at all the beautiful things around you!" he called out to me on a sunny Saturday morning as we were sitting on the back porch together. He pointed to the bright-orange marigolds scattered throughout the rock garden and the cheery little red and yellow finches in the birdfeeder. While normally my favorite place ever, I'd been so weepy that summer I'd hardly noticed.

But Matt didn't stop there. He went on to list the many examples of God's goodness in our lives—despite the suffering and sorrows we'd been through—and he was right. God's goodness was abundantly evident everywhere around us. Yet I'd lost sight of it with the recent and unrelenting trials we'd been experiencing.

Perhaps you've been there. Maybe you're there right now and you're struggling to find much—if any—goodness around you. As you can tell, I know that struggle.

So then you can see why the word *goodness* would jump out at me while I was studying the fruits of the Spirit. *Goodness:* There it was folded so softly between kindness and faithfulness that I'd hardly paid it any mind. But I was paying attention now.

I wanted to know, what is the actual meaning of the word *goodness*? And what place does it have in our life and marriage?

For starters, *goodness* means *doing* what is right, whether we feel like it or not and, even more challenging, whether the other person warrants it or not. It's a readiness to do good wherever we have opportunity. True goodness isn't about a feeling ("I'm feeling good today") but typically involves a sacrificial action, big or small. It's a loving choice. Simply put, we *decide* to show goodness—just as God our Father often shows us overwhelming goodness when we least deserve it.

So, we can practice goodness in our marriage, and we can *look* for goodness too. Remember our back-porch conversation? The one where I was blind to the beauties of the garden and the cheerfulness of the chirping birds? I didn't notice them because *I wasn't looking*. Goodness was everywhere around me, yet I was missing it because I didn't have eyes to see. I was more focused on what had been lost rather than what was also *found* during that difficult time.

Sometimes it's like that in marriage. We lose sight of the goodness right in front of us because we're too caught up in our trials and disappointments. So, if that's where you're at today, ask God to help you see His good gifts that surround you. You might be surprised to learn that there is far more goodness in your life—in your marriage—than you first believed.

Reflection

- What are the many ways God has been good to you over the months and years?
- If you were to stop and look around today, what goodness would you be able to see in your marriage?

Application

Get out a fresh piece of paper and write the word *Goodness* at the top. Then, underneath that word, start listing all that is *good* in your life and your marriage. And it's fine to start with the small things—holding hands, saying grace, locking up the house at night—and then keep going from there.

You might also find the book of Psalms to be a rich reminder of God's goodness toward us. Here are only a few examples: Psalms 23:6; 31:19; and 34:8.

Prayer

Dear Heavenly Father, I'm grateful for Your goodness to me. Would You please open my eyes to all that is right and good everywhere around me? Help me to see the good— and to do good—in my marriage. In Jesus's name, amen.

34

Worship

> But the hour is coming, and now is, when the true worshipers will worship the Father in spirit and truth; for the Father is seeking such to worship Him. God is Spirit, and those who worship Him must worship in spirit and truth.
>
> John 4:23–24 NKJV

The first time I found Matt lying flat on his home office floor, I gasped, fearing the worst.

"It's okay, hon, I'm just worshiping the Lord," he reassured me as if that short statement was sufficient explanation. But it wasn't enough for me. After all, who in their right mind lies facedown on the floor for worship? Other than my husband, of course.

Because that's not my idea of worship. When I hear that word, my mind goes to the four-hour-long Spotify playlist I listen to most every morning—the one I've literally named (not so creatively) "My Worship." I love singing along with my favorite praise and worship songs as I prepare for the day.

And although I view singing as a legitimate way to worship, I'll concede it's not the same as burying your face in the carpet. So I had to ask myself, Do I prefer the more pleasant forms of worship but avoid the humble bow? A question worth considering.

How about you? What does *worship* look like for you? Perhaps you play or sing loud praise songs to God. You dance or maybe kneel. You go to the Saturday night hymn sing or attend a Sunday morning worship service. Then again, perhaps you're like Matt and worship silently with your face humbly on the ground.

But what does *worship* mean? Surprisingly, even though I am a seminary graduate, I had never spent much time studying worship, nor what it might look like in my life and marriage. But after seeing Matt on the floor, I was intrigued.

My study started with the basics, such as researching how the word *worship* is defined and described in the Bible. For instance, did you know that the Old Testament word for worship, *šāḥâ*, quite literally means "to bow down, to prostrate oneself" or "to lay flat on the ground"?[1] I didn't. Furthermore, the New Testament *worship* has a similar meaning: "to fall on your knees" or "prostrate yourself in homage or as an act of reverence."[2] So, apparently, my husband wasn't as overboard as I first believed.

This is not to say you're required to fall on the floor to worship the Lord. Yet you can see it's reasonable to consider the possibility. At the very least, it's worth taking a second look at *how* and *when* we worship.

Now, if that's the *what* of worship—a bowing or kneeling in reverence—then what about the *when* of worship? I suspect many of us view worship as something primarily reserved for Sunday, while the rest of our week goes on in a blur of work, children, chores, and too much screen time. But, oh friend, if this is all our week holds, then we are truly missing out on a privilege, as well as how we're called to live as Christians.

No matter how busy or preoccupied you may be, I hope you won't pass up the many opportunities to worship the Lord throughout your day. When you wake up in the morning, pause for a minute to acknowledge His greatness instead of starting to scroll social media. Maybe fall on your face or get down on your knees. Sing softly of His goodness while you rock your baby. In the evening, join your husband in bowing before God to thank Him for the day and the blessings He's bestowed.

Can you imagine the difference this kind of devoted worship would make in how you view your current circumstances and daily challenges? How it might impact your relationships and even your marriage? (I can testify from personal experience that it's not easy to remain upset with your husband while worshiping the Lord!) And, best of all, how worship will deepen your walk with God?

Reflection

- Describe your personal expression of worship to the Lord. When do you worship?
- In what ways do you think your worship experience might affect your marriage?

Application

Take some time over the next few days to reflect on what it means to worship and, more importantly, *why* as believers we're called to worship. Then perhaps write out *when, where,* and *why* you worship, including anything you believe the Spirit is leading you to do differently after prayer and reflection.

Then, for a bonus assignment, try looking up the many verses about worship, first in the Old Testament and then in the New Testament. And if you notice any patterns or themes developing, jot those down too. What do you observe, and how might that apply to your life as well? Here are a few of my favorites to get you started: Psalm 95:6; Isaiah 12:5; Romans 12:1; and Colossians 3:14–17.

Prayer

Dear Heavenly Father, I desire to worship You "in Spirit and truth" (John 4:24). And I don't want to merely save it for Sunday, but instead, I want to make worshiping You an important part of my daily life. You are worthy of my praise and worship. In Jesus's name, amen.

35

Thankfulness

I give thanks to my God always for you because of the grace of God that was given you in Christ Jesus.

1 Corinthians 1:4

My friend's happiness shone through every word of her short text message to me: "My husband and I had a small conflict when we first arrived but resolved it quickly, and ever since, we've enjoyed a really peaceful and joyful vacation together!" She was downright jubilant. Then, as visible proof of their current state of bliss, she included a picture of them wrapped up in a close embrace in front of a splashing blue ocean.

Once my friend returned home from their beautiful beach holiday, I was eager to hear more of the story behind her victory text and accompanying photo, and she gladly filled me in.

When she and her husband left for their trip, they were aware that it would be more of a working vacation than a typical family holiday. They agreed that their days would be spent with him attending business meetings at a nearby hotel conference center while she was holidaying with their kids back at their vacation rental. He'd return for the evening, and then, after the conference was over, they'd all enjoy a few fun days together down at the beach.

But what might have sounded like a good plan beforehand turned out to be impractical once on the ground. Because on the very first night after their arrival, her husband texted to say he would stay over at the hotel rather than returning to the rental as originally intended. This left his wife on her own to care for the children in a strange town—far from the semi-holiday she'd envisioned.

Now, for him, this text was merely an FYI, but for her, it was a trigger that sent her spiraling down, down, down. So, after she tucked the kids in for the night, she slipped to her room to pour out her heart before the Lord. Then she began rehearsing her hurts—reaching far back to early marriage days and similar past offenses. Tears flowed as she thought of the many other times she'd been let down over the years.

And then, out of nowhere (as she explained later), she felt an impulse to grab the notebook on her nightstand. She flipped to a fresh page and on the top, she wrote, "Ten Things I Love about My Husband." And she slowly started writing one quality after another—until she got stuck about halfway through. But refusing to give up, she pushed through to come up with the last five to complete her list of ten.

Still, she wasn't done. Her next step was to read and reread her list to herself, letting each one sink into her soul. And, by the time she turned out the light, she drifted off with a heart full of love and gratitude. Such a testimony of how a woman can overcome her spiraling negative thoughts—with something as simple as a lined notebook and ballpoint pen.

And how I could relate! How many times has some random text, careless comment, or thoughtless act by my husband sent me reeling? Started me on the spiral? So many times. And I'd later regret having wasted precious time and ruining wonderful holidays with my determination to focus on what was wrong . . . rather than dwelling on what was right.

Maybe that's your struggle too. The triggers, the spirals, the resentments. That list of offenses never too far away when something else sets you off.

If so, then consider my friend's story. By choosing to meditate on what was pure, lovely, and good in their marriage (see Phil. 4:8 NKJV), she was able to enjoy *peace and joy*—and happy laughter and warm embraces—in the time they had left on their holiday together.

And that's true for you and me as well. So let's choose to think on these things.

> Finally, brethren, whatever things are true, whatever things are noble, whatever things are just, whatever things are pure, whatever things are lovely, whatever things are of good report, if there is any virtue and if there is anything praiseworthy—*meditate on these things.* (Phil. 4:8 NKJV)

Reflection

- Do you spend more time thinking about those things you appreciate about your husband or focusing on his faults and disappointments?
- What is something you could name about him right now that you're thankful for?

Application

To be clear, neither this story nor the following exercise is intended to obscure or avoid working out hurts and offenses in your marriage. (For instance, my friend and her husband did eventually discuss their holiday situation but later, in a healthy way, with grace and fairness.) So, with that in mind this week, focus on those things for which you're thankful.

How about starting with what you enjoy about your husband? What do you admire about him? What do you love about him? Then pull out your notebook and write out ten (or more!) things you appreciate about him.

But don't limit this exercise to this week. Instead, consider making it a regular practice in the weeks, months, and years ahead. Such a list turned around my friend's entire holiday. Imagine what making this a regular habit could do for your marriage!

Prayer

Dear Lord, I want to grow in my thankfulness for my husband. Help me to see and remember what is good and right about him—to focus on the good things he says and does over the negative. I desire to be a thankful wife. In Jesus's name, amen.

36

Holiness

But as He who called you is holy, you also be holy in all your conduct, because it is written, "Be holy, for I am holy."

1 Peter 1:15–16 NKJV

The series started out innocently enough. Most people would even describe it as downright wholesome. And so, several times a week, after the kids were in bed, we'd curl up together to watch an episode of our newfound show. Funny, charming, laced with a bit of mystery—it had everything we were looking for at the time.

Yet, as the series continued, the show began introducing a few additional—and for us, unexpected and unwanted—elements, such as a brief extramarital affair and other suggestive scenes. We decided to overlook it at first, hoping they would get back to that fresh storytelling we had initially enjoyed. But the program kept going farther and farther down a questionable road that we had hoped to avoid.

Then one night, smack in the middle of an exciting cliff-hanger episode, Matt shut his computer and softly said, "We can't watch this anymore."

And I knew he was right. As much as I'd been enjoying the series, I had felt increasingly uncomfortable with the content, knowing it was a compromise to what we believed. Perhaps not horrific compared to others, but neither was it in keeping with basic biblical standards.

Now please understand: Matt and I are neither uptight nor legalistic about such things. We watch and appreciate many popular shows (often viewed through VidAngel, a streaming service that allows users to filter out inappropriate content), but we're also committed to what God has called us to do—and that is to walk in *holiness*.

The Bible explicitly tells the believer that you are to be "holy in all your conduct" (1 Pet. 1:15). Such a small handful of words, but full of great significance to our daily lives.

So, let's take a closer look at several of these words, starting with *holy*. The Greek word for *holy* is *hagios*, and it means a "most holy thing" or "a saint."[1] Above all, it signifies being separated and, in this case, separated from sin—separated and sacred.

Next, let's consider the word *all*, which in Greek is *pas*. Can you guess what that one means? You're right; in addition to "all," it means "everything."[2] No exceptions.

Then finally, there's the Greek word for *conduct*, *anastrophē*, which refers to your manner of life or how you behave. It's what you choose to do and how you comport yourself.[3]

So, put it all together and that instruction to "be holy in all your conduct" is saying that, as children of God, we are to be set apart *from* sin and to be set apart *for* God. In everything we do. Every day of our lives.

Rather sobering, isn't it? And so it should be. Yet, let's not lose sight of a couple of things. The first is that if our kind and sovereign God has called us to do something, He will equip and enable us to do what He has asked. Second, we can give our attention to the first half of holiness—that which we are set apart *from*—or we can balance it out with the second half of holiness—that which we are set apart *for*. Because when those two halves are put together, the *from* and the *for*, it makes for a beautiful picture of sacred love.

Wholesome and holy. Right and true.

As believers in Christ, we have a choice when it comes to holiness. We can view it as a heavy and impossible calling or as a light and freeing one. We can be weighed down by what we "can't" do or delight in what we were made to enjoy. It's up to you. But my hope is that you will consider the pursuit of holiness as something of a joy and blessing for your marriage.

Reflection

- How have you pursued holiness in your marriage?
- In what specific ways has God called you to be holy as a wife?

Application

Because we serve a holy God, holiness is a prominent theme found throughout the Bible. Consider taking this week to study the word *holiness* and reflect on its meaning in your life and marriage. Here are a few verses I encourage you to look up in your Bible so you can read them in their complete context: Romans 12:1; 2 Corinthians 7:1; and Hebrews 12:14.

As you study and reflect on our calling to be holy, write down the characteristics of holiness. What do you hear God calling you to be set apart *from*? And what do you see as God calling you *for*? If your husband is willing to have the conversation, sit down together and talk through what that means for your marriage too.

Prayer

Dear Heavenly Father, I know You are a holy God and have called us to enjoy a holy marriage. Please give my husband and me wisdom in making good decisions together for what we allow into our lives. Help us to walk in holiness. In Jesus's name, amen.

37

Grace

Let your speech always be with grace, seasoned with salt, that you may know how you ought to answer each one.

Colossians 4:6 NKJV

know many couples who have discovered a shared hobby. For some, it's hiking, sailing, or tennis; for others, it might be bowling, dancing, or bird-watching. For Matt and me, it happens to be cooking. We both enjoy creating all kinds of dishes in the kitchen, each in our individual style.

And I don't think you'll be too surprised when I say that I'm the type of cook who adheres to the recipe *precisely*. I order the exact ingredients, carefully measure out each one, and closely follow the directions, step-by-step.

Matt, on the other hand, is inclined to go off-script. Oh, he'll assure you he's making it just like Chef John and will pull up his YouTube channel to prove it. But if pressed, he'll probably confess that he might have substituted a few ingredients . . . and fudged a few of the steps. The man can't help himself. But whatever he's making, strictly Chef John or not, one thing you can count on: He will double, or even triple, the amount of spices.

And that right there is our biggest source of dispute—and laughter—in the kitchen. For me, a teaspoon is a *teaspoon*; for him, a teaspoon is a *tablespoon*.

Let's just say that if you came over and agreed to a blindfolded taste-test of one of our home-cooked meals, I'm confident you'd immediately guess *who* made *which* recipe. If the dish has a soft, subtle flavor, that one would be mine. However, if your eyes water and you exhale a few small flames, that would be Matt's masterpiece. And even though I hope you would conclude that both dishes are delicious, my guess is that you would find his so much more than that—his dish would be *memorable*.

Then he would declare it's all in the seasoning.

So this is but one of the reasons I'm intrigued by the above verse in Colossians—the one that says our speech is to "be full of grace" and "seasoned with salt." As an (aspiring) amateur cook, I'm keenly aware of the difference a good seasoning can make to what is being served. Although you don't have to be Julia Child to recognize that! We've all tasted something we found particularly delightful, thanks to the careful touch by the chef who created it.

And so it is with our speech, according to Scripture. What we have to say—and how it is received—can often come down to how we've chosen to *season* it.

Consider the communication in your marriage. What do you do when you have something sensitive to say? Something difficult to discuss? Do you take time and care to "season your speech" before diving in, or do you blurt it out? Personally, I've tried both ways. And maybe you have too. But wouldn't you agree that the conversation goes so much better when you've taken the trouble to say it *with grace*?

Now let's take a closer look at *grace* and its meaning, especially in the context of this verse in Colossians. The Greek word used is *charis*, and the first definition is "that which affords joy, pleasure, delight, sweetness, charm, loveliness; grace of speech."[1] How striking to see so many beautiful words right in a row!

So then, if you stopped to evaluate your marriage communication—both *what* you say and *how* you say it—does it align with the above description? Is it *full* of those things like sweetness, charm, and loveliness?

Next, there's the expression "seasoned with salt." Here the word *season* is literally the same word used for preparing food or "to make savory."[2] In other words, if you catch yourself about to say something negative or harsh, take a breath and remember this verse. Then try adding a generous amount of grace along with a dash of wisdom to make your message more palatable.

Reflection

- Would you describe your speech as "full of grace"? How about "seasoned with salt"?
- What kind of difference do you think it would make if you carefully seasoned your speech, specifically in your marriage?

Application

As you reflect on your marriage relationship, are you beginning to suspect your speech has been seasoned with a bit too much "pepper" (and you can guess what I mean by that!) and not enough "salt"? If so and you'd like to change that, it might be helpful to identify what you do and *don't* want to mark your communication with your husband.

Try dividing a sheet of paper into two columns. On one side, list those ingredients that have no place in your speech, such as sarcasm, sass, sharpness, or bitterness (you can look up Eph. 4:31 for others). And then, in the other column, write out your preferred "spices," such as kindness, cheerfulness, softness, and joy. Then pray and ask God to fill your heart and speech with the qualities in that second column.

Prayer

Dear Lord, I want whatever comes out of my mouth to be full of grace and seasoned with salt. Fill me with Your Spirit so that my speech is heavily seasoned with delight and joy. I desire to be a wise, gracious, and truthful wife. In Jesus's name, amen.

38

Peacemaker

Blessed are the peacemakers.

Matthew 5:9 NKJV

didn't realize I was a runner until after I was married. And by that, I don't mean I run three miles a day no matter what the weather. What I mean is that wherever I encountered conflict, my impulse was to run—to *get out of there* as a way to avoid strife or contention.

And I was a fairly successful runner . . . up until I married Matt Jacobson.

That's when things started to change, beginning with one particular argument we had early on in our marriage. I wouldn't even describe it as a big blowup (because it wasn't), but what made it so significant was how I handled the situation. As I had no interest in discussing the issue any further and Matt wasn't about to let it go, I did what I instinctively do in this sort of scenario: I grabbed the car keys and drove away.

Just like that. In the early evening, pregnant with our first child, driving off into the dark. Running away. *Conflict avoided.*

However, when I returned to our apartment later that night, the lights were still on, and Matt was waiting up for me—quiet, calm, and loving—and with the most serious look I'd ever seen on his face.

"Babe, running away cannot be one of our options. We can take timeouts and we can temporarily put quarrels aside, but let's decide right here and now that we will have a work-it-out marriage."

And I knew he was right. Perhaps I had successfully avoided conflict that evening, but I also understood that my impulse to run away from difficult discussions would never bring about the peace I truly desired.

Ever since I was a young girl, my mother referred to me as "the peacemaker," so it's evidently part of my personality and gifting. The problem, however, was that I equated "conflict averted" with "peace made"—never realizing there was a difference.

And maybe you're the same. Are you, like me, a runner? Inclined to avoid conflict wherever possible? I'm with you. Yet, in the process, we're not actually achieving our goal of peace. Instead, we're merely avoiding the inevitable and, furthermore, will likely make things worse over time with our unhealthy approach to disagreement.

But maybe you're not a runner, and conflict doesn't bother you; it might even energize you. Perhaps you're a bring-it-on kind of person who doesn't want to leave the room until you've resolved the situation or—less helpful—until you've gotten in the last word.

If so, here I'd offer an alternative word of caution. Don't assume that running headlong into conflict is the only or the best way to work things out. In your marriage, peace might call for the opposite; instead, you'd do well to bite back your remarks, refrain from argument, or, as frustrating as it may be, wait patiently for him to (more slowly) process an issue. And backing off might be as much a challenge for you as leaning in is for someone like me.

Whichever your approach to conflict—conflict avoider, conflict energizer, or something in between—let me challenge you to consider the level of peace in your relationship. Is your marriage marked by tension? Filled with frequent bickering, strife, or contention? If so, you'll want to seriously consider *why* that is—not looking to blame the other person but being willing to identify the ways you might be contributing to the discord in your marriage.

Perhaps you've sidestepped important issues, and now it's time to do the hard work of working it out. Or maybe you've been too ready to stir it up or blow it up, and you need to grow in your skills as a peacemaker. Either way, go forward and, as the Bible says, "pursue the things which make for peace" (Rom. 14:19 NKJV).

Reflection

- What is your natural reaction when you encounter conflict? Do you run away? Do you take a head-on approach?
- In which areas or situations of your marriage would you like to see more peace?

Application

Spend time this week reflecting on the specific ways you can be a peacemaker in your marriage.

You can take out your notebook and draw two columns: one with the things you do *not* want to do (e.g., bicker, argue, or run away) and another with what you *will* do (e.g., agree, accept, or stay to work it out) to bring more peace into your relationship. Then, after you've made and looked over your list, pick one or two areas you want to work on in your role as a peacemaker in your marriage. And, friend, remember, "blessed are the peacemakers" (Matt. 5:9 NKJV).

Prayer

Dear Heavenly Father, I desire the blessings of being a peacemaker. Show me how I can bring more peace into my marriage with what I say or don't say, what I do or don't do. Give me the strength to stay, the determination to work it out, and the wisdom to know what is needed so we can enjoy a healthy, peace-filled relationship. In Jesus's name, amen.

39

Covenant

I have made a covenant with my eyes.
How then could I look at a young woman?

Job 31:1 CSB

never meant to eavesdrop. The only reason I happened to overhear their conversation was because I'd softly tiptoed into the house in case my in-laws were catching a nap on that warm summer afternoon.

But I could see they weren't sleeping. Instead, I found the two of them lovingly holding hands across the kitchen table, quietly talking together—enjoying one of my mother-in-law's brief moments of clarity. By then, Alzheimer's had made it so she rarely recognized her husband of sixty-plus years. Yet, on that afternoon, she knew who he was all right, and was as much in love as when they'd first married. Possibly more so.

And that's how I came to overhear this precious conversation. The two of them were discussing Mom's passing, with

Mom observing that she didn't believe she had much time left. She'd be "heading home" soon—a phrase often used while wandering in those last months and years—except this time when she said it, it was plain that she meant her home in heaven. Dad didn't reply or try to deny it; he simply squeezed her tender hand a little tighter.

Then she looked up into his dear blue eyes and told him, "I wish I could tie a strong, thick rope from me to you, and you could come up with me when I go. Then we wouldn't ever be parted."

And I could hear Dad chuckling at the thought of that picture. Followed by a long moment of silence. The two of them soberly reflecting on the fact that they would soon be separated for the first time in sixty-three years.

I've often thought of these two, now enjoying the glories of heaven—with or without a rope to tie them together—and how this preciousness at the end came from great perseverance and commitment. And I've contemplated how many times they could have given up—some might even say *should have* given up. How they were too young when they got married (with her at seventeen and him at nineteen). Or how they didn't start out as Christians and both came into the marriage with much sin, trauma, and, believe me, plenty of baggage.

No one would've guessed they'd make it six years, let alone sixty.

Yet Matt's parents were committed to their wedding vows. They understood they had made a *covenant* before God, and it meant that they would stay together "'til death do them part" and always be true to one another. More than a mere wish or a deep desire, a covenant is an unbreakable promise, a binding agreement. This is not some casual agreement but a strong and lasting vow that changes *everything*. And this is how, by way of the marriage covenant, two people mysteriously, and yet truly, become one (Eph. 5:25–33).

A covenant to keep. A covenant to cultivate. A covenant to protect.

And so it is my hope that Matt and I, too, will still be holding hands at the end of our days together. I wish the same for you as well.

Reflection

- Do you think of your marriage as a true covenant—a sacred vow to keep?
- What are some of the ways you protect and preserve your marriage vows?

Application

Consider spending some time this week researching and reflecting on the meaning of *covenant*, particularly as it's found throughout the Bible. Here are but a few examples to get you started (you'll want to look up each verse for context):

- "God remembered his *covenant*" (Exod. 2:24).
- "I will not violate my *covenant*" (Ps. 89:34).
- "'This is my *covenant* with them,' says the LORD" (Isa. 59:21).
- "Even with a man-made *covenant*, no one annuls it or adds to it once it has been ratified" (Gal. 3:15).

After you look up these verses (and a simple search on the word *covenant* will help you find others), write down anything you observe about *who* is making the covenant and *why*. What do you see that might apply to your own marriage covenant?

Next, you might want to pull out your own marriage vows if it's been a while since you've thought about what you pledged together. Perhaps contact a calligrapher and ask them to write out your vows, then frame them to put up in your home as a visual reminder of your covenant.

Another idea is to set aside a special night to reread your vows to each other. It can be as simple as a nice dinner at home or perhaps you'll want to invite a few close friends and family over as "witnesses" for both encouragement and accountability.

Last, you might want to plan a special ceremony to renew your vows formally. I've seen this done in so many beautiful and creative ways! While not essential, it can be a powerful reminder and renewal of your lasting love for one another.

Prayer

Dear Heavenly Father, I have made a sacred covenant with my husband before You. Help me not only to keep my vows but to protect and value them. Please renew and refresh our hearts for each other. In Jesus's name, amen.

Note: God's Word is also abundantly clear that He deeply cares about your safety and well-being. If you feel you are in any way in danger or at risk, please seek professional help from a qualified biblical counselor or from legal counsel.

40

Remembering

Remember the former things of old;
for I am God, and there is no other;
I am God, and there is none like me.

Isaiah 46:9

For a long time, I wondered if there might be something wrong with me.

We'd have guests over for dinner, and nearly everyone around the table would have seemingly endless childhood memories to share. But not me. Oh, I could come up with a handful or two but comparatively few. And yet I had a reasonably normal childhood with as many adventures and experiences as the next person. So, what was that about?

The answer is likely layered, but one theory is that I've always been quick—far too quick—to move on to the next thing. That is to say, before the current event was complete, I was already looking ahead to the following one. Perhaps there are worse things, but this march-on approach can turn life into a bit of a blur. And, unfortunately, my husband is much the same way. Between the two of us, we're continually pushing forward and carrying on. And drive can be healthy. But now we have a few regrets about so much push.

We regret that we haven't been mindful of cementing more memories over the years. That we didn't stop long enough to reflect on and celebrate the many extraordinary—as well as the wonderfully ordinary—events in our marriage and family. I can see now how memories can play such an important role in a relationship.

And it was for this reason that when a good friend suggested I put together a photo book for Matt's sixtieth birthday, I jumped at the idea. I've wanted to tackle such an album for years but never got around to it in our nearly three decades of marriage. (For that matter, I still haven't finished our wedding album. Yes, it's *that* bad.)

But this time, it would be different. I determined that this gift would be something to remember. So I scrolled through hundreds of photos we had to choose from, and all the while, this particular phrase ran through my mind: *I am a memory maker.* An exciting—and sobering—prospect. To think, I get to both *make* and *keep* memories. I have the privilege and opportunity to lovingly document our lives together.

As do you. What a strong role you, as a wife, have to play! You can create memories for both of you to look back on for the rest of your years together.

Furthermore, you can choose which ones to highlight and which ones are better left behind—and a wise woman knows which ones are which. You can keep throwing past mistakes and disappointments into the conversation, *or* you can recall that time he got it right. You can reminisce over the good times you've shared, *or* you can rehearse that old, familiar argument between you two. Can't you feel the power in that?

So, sister, take a moment to consider what kind of memory maker you want to be. And if, like me, you have some regrets about how you've gone about it in the past, don't let it discourage you. Just think: Today is a blank day with plenty of fresh opportunities to make new and beautiful memories.

Reflection

- Are you mindful of the memories you're making together in your marriage?
- Do you spend much time pondering and reflecting on the good work God has done in your lives?

Application

Consider putting together a special photo album, as I did, of the past year's (or many years') highlights. Another idea is to search for a special keepsake box and begin collecting notes, souvenirs, and other memorabilia. Then perhaps start a tradition where you sit down and sift through the box each year together. Make it an evening to laugh, cry, and remember!

Sometimes memory-making is as much about forgetting as it is remembering. For example, do you tend to bring up old fights or bitter memories—even though long ago dealt with and (supposedly) forgiven—to stir up strife or hold over his head? Decide to bury those resentments for good and focus on the bright spots instead.

Prayer

My God and Savior, I want to "ponder the work of Your hands" (Ps. 143:5) in my marriage. Help us to see the good You've done and to treasure the memories we've made and the ones to come as well. In Jesus's name, amen.

41

Generosity

One gives freely, yet grows all the richer;
  another withholds what he should give, and
    only suffers want.
Whoever brings blessing will be enriched,
  and one who waters will himself be watered.

Proverbs 11:24–25

In our home, I am affectionately known as "the Budget Queen." And there's a reason for that: I love saving money, finding a good deal, and cutting costs. I don't know about you, but this kind of careful economizing brings me an inexplicable sense of satisfaction.

My husband, on the other hand, leans toward lavish; he's not nearly as concerned about cost or expense.

Don't misunderstand; Matt is mindful of the budget. But if you were going to get a gift from one of us, he's definitely the one you should pick. Trust me. Because he'll look for the most fantastic present we can afford—maybe even a bit beyond that—and you won't be sorry.

While I can say that I now appreciate Matt's extravagant tendencies, even genuinely admire them, it wasn't always so. Earlier on in our marriage, I didn't necessarily agree with his generous impulses and was convinced that my strict budgeting was a better, wiser, and, let's face it, more *biblical* approach.

Not anymore. Over the years, I've come to recognize that what I've called "economizing" can often merely be an excuse for being "miserly." *Ouch*.

And before you conclude that I'm being too hard on myself when it comes to this budget stuff, here's what changed my perspective—when I started looking at our Heavenly Father and how He is toward us. After all, is God tightfisted and "careful" with us? Is He a minimalist when it comes to His gifts? Or is God incredibly *lavish* with His love and blessings?

If you are a believer, then you already know the answer to that question. What wonderful love is lavished on us that we should be called *the children of God* (see 1 John 3:1)! But it doesn't stop there. The Bible also tells us that He is "able to do exceedingly abundantly above all that we ask or think" (Eph. 3:20 NKJV). In short—think *sheer extravagance*.

And if this is God's way toward us, how can it not inspire us to respond similarly toward our spouse? Why would we continue to give the bare minimum when we've been showered "exceedingly abundantly"?

Yes, *why*? Maybe you struggle to give generously of your time, money, or attention because others—whether family, friends, or people from church—haven't always been so kind to you, and it doesn't feel wise or safe. Maybe you don't feel as though you have much (more) to give. Or perhaps you're just prone to selfishness, paying more attention to what is "due" you than what you can offer. In any case, consider your *why*, but then decide if you want to grow in this area of generosity.

And if you desire to grow, a good place to start is by remembering how generous your Heavenly Father has been with you. Think of the many ways He has been good to you—His bountiful gifts, His unbelievable blessings, and His many kindnesses toward you.

Maybe read up on what else the Bible says about God's lavish love and gifts. Here are but a few of my favorite passages: Psalm 86:15; Zephaniah 3:17; Romans 5:8; and 1 John 3:1. Look up each one and read it aloud, inserting your name or "me" where possible.

For example: "The LORD [my] God is in [my] midst, a mighty one who will save; he will rejoice over [me] with gladness; he will quiet [me] by his love; he will exult over [me] with loud singing" (Zeph. 3:17). It's almost overwhelming, isn't it?

And if that's God's heart for us, that's the same kind of spirit we can have toward others, but especially toward our husbands. So why not start on a wild and lavish love-showering spree?

Reflection

- Have you spent much time considering how great the Father's love is for you? Or thinking about His abundant gifts to you?
- And with His example in mind, how generous are you with your time, gifts, and other expressions of love for your husband?

Application

What are some of the specific ways you can demonstrate your extravagant love for your husband? It doesn't necessarily need to be an expensive present; it could be a generous gift of your time or a thoughtful gesture or an offering of special attention. And don't hesitate to get carried away; write down as many ideas as come to mind. Then enjoy showering your husband with an elaborate expression of your love for him!

Prayer

Dear Heavenly Father, my heart is full of gratitude for the lavish love You've bestowed on me! I'm thankful for the many beautiful gifts I did not ask for and Your loving kindnesses I did not deserve. Please help me to generously express my love toward my husband. In Jesus's name, amen.

42

Submission

Now as the church submits to Christ, so also wives should submit in everything to their husbands.

Ephesians 5:24

First of all, I'll own that I have no excuse; I was hardly raised in a bubble. I've made my home in Southern California, Tennessee, and Oregon and, when I was single, studied and traveled in Europe, Africa, and the Middle East. And, in addition to being involved in church most of my life, I happen to hold a seminary degree.

So who knows how I managed to skip over the verses on submission in the Bible. Because it wasn't until after we were married that I noticed this astonishing Scripture. I remember the occasion well: There I was, curled up on the couch, making my way through the book of Ephesians for my morning devotions when suddenly it popped out at me.

Wives, submit to your own husbands, as to the Lord. (Eph. 5:22)

Now, surely, I'd read that same verse hundreds of times in those many years I'd attended church and studied in seminary, and yet it might as well have been the first time I'd seen it. I looked up to stare wonderingly at my husband, busy frying up eggs for our breakfast, and it was as if I was seeing him for the first time too.

I glanced back down at my Bible and then back up at him. And that's the moment I grasped that God was talking to *me*—about *him*.

Here the Bible was instructing me to honor him, to defer to him, and to follow him, and yet—I have to be honest with you—this concept went against nearly everything I had absorbed in the previous years. As in, diametrically opposed. Antithetical. Worlds clashing.

I'd learned plenty about self-reliance and self-respect in my studies and travels, and I had learned those lessons well, but this concept of *submission?* Not so much. Not at all.

So I immediately dove into a word study. I wanted to know what the Bible actually meant by *submit.* The word in Greek is *hypotassō* and means "put under" or "be subject to"[1]— reasonably straightforward. However, what was more helpful was to learn that it's also a Greek military term meaning "to arrange [troop divisions] in a military fashion under the command of a leader."[2] Or, in nonmilitary use, it's "a voluntary attitude of giving in, cooperating, assuming responsibility, and carrying a burden."[3]

Under command. Giving in. A responsibility. And, possibly, *a burden to carry.*

Wow. I had some serious thinking to do. No, more than thinking, this called for wrestling. How do you respond when the Word of God instructs you to do something contrary to what has been poured into you for years? *Wrestle.*

So, how about you? Have you wrestled with this subject? Do you know that feeling when you learn what is required—what the Bible clearly instructs—and yet it seems to go against everything around you? Maybe against everything *inside* you?

I'm with you, sister. But I also know that, as followers of Christ, we're called to obey His Word even if it is completely out of step with our culture or our comfort zone. So now, if you haven't done so already, this might be the time to start wrestling with what submission means for your marriage.

Reflection

- What kind of reaction or response do you have when you hear the biblical word *submission*?
- Have you wrestled with what it looks like to submit to your husband?

Application

You might find it helpful to do a further study of the passage in Ephesians 5, beginning with verse 22 and going to the end of the chapter. Take notes as you go through it, observing *who* is being addressed (wives, husbands, Christ, or the church), *what* is being said, and *why*.

And if you've never grappled with what God's instruction looks like for you in your marriage, pray and ask Him to show you what He'd have you do. Maybe you'll want to write out your questions, objections, and concerns, as well as your convictions.

You've probably noticed that I've not spelled out any specifics for this subject. That's because I don't believe there's a formula or checklist; I only believe there's a Holy Spirit, and I trust Him to reveal what needs to be revealed. And while I don't think *submission* means simply saying, "Yes, dear" (Matt and I certainly don't have that kind of relationship!), it does mean *something*—and that's for you to wrestle with before the Lord.

Last, if you've done the study above, you'll have noticed that the Scripture passage in Ephesians also distinctly addresses husbands. You'll find powerful words such as *love* and *cherish* when it comes to how he is to treat you. And if your husband is reading the companion devotional, *Loving Your Wife Well*, then you can count on him being heavily challenged as well. But— and this is important—don't make your obedience dependent on his obedience. Just pay attention to what God is asking you to do, and trust Him to take care of your husband.

Prayer

Dear Heavenly Father, I'm committed to obeying Your Word—the easy parts and the hard parts. Show me what it means to submit to my husband, and give me the grace and strength to do it. I pray that we will enjoy a healthy, godly marriage together. In Jesus's name, amen.

Note: While "submit" is a biblical instruction, God's Word is also abundantly clear that He deeply cares about your safety and well-being. If you feel you are in any way in danger or at risk, please seek professional help from a qualified biblical counselor or from legal counsel.

43

Trauma

Some moments are forever imprinted on your mind. Hauntingly etched there, never to be forgotten. One such event occurred in our lives more than sixteen years ago, though it's as vivid in my memory as if it happened only yesterday.

Even now, if I close my eyes, I can still hear the crunch of tiny bones and feel the warm stickiness of blood staining my favorite white blouse.

We never saw it coming. The day started so marvelously—an exceptionally fine Fourth of July—and our entire family was celebrating out in the front yard. Matt decided to show the older children how to do a headstand out on the grass while I cheered him on from the porch steps, our nearly one-year-old son sitting close by. Everyone was laughing and clapping, and I was so caught up in the fun of it that I never noticed the baby slipping from his spot next to me and making a beeline for Daddy.

While we're not clear what exactly happened that afternoon, what we do know is that Matt suddenly lost his balance and all of his 230 pounds landed squarely on our little one. And our family laughter turned to terrified screaming with everyone crying—everyone that is, except for the baby.

He lay motionless on the grass. Where there was blood. *A pool of blood.*

I could never adequately describe what happened next because I've never seen my husband respond the way he did after that horrific accident. But if you've ever seen or heard *anguish*, then maybe you can imagine it. My husband was convinced he'd just killed his baby boy and, truly, it was more than that daddy's heart could take.

In the middle of all that chaos, I ran across the lawn to scoop up our baby, terrified of what I'd find. Thankfully, I discovered he was still breathing, but it was also obvious that he urgently needed medical help.

We bothered with neither car seat nor speed limit, as we drove our injured baby to the hospital. There we learned, thankfully, that the crunch we heard was not his neck or skull after all (as Matt had first believed) but our child's teeth and jaw. Although a severe injury, it was not a life-threatening one.

And can you believe that same "baby" is now seventeen years old, and you'd never guess he'd been in such a serious accident? He doesn't even remember anything from that eventful day. My husband and I, on the other hand, will never forget it. The terror of the moment. The rush to the hospital. The grief. The guilt. The relief. *All of it.*

What does a couple do when faced with devastating trauma, no matter the outcome? A tragic accident, an unexpected phone call, a grim diagnosis, a heartbreaking loss—that life-changing moment that came out of nowhere. How do you walk through heartbreak together?

I have no simple outline for you to follow, but one thing I do know is that you can always cry out to God. When you don't know what else to do or where else to turn—*lament*. Express your deep regret, grief, or sorrow—just like the emotions you come across over and over again throughout the book of Psalms. Write it out. Cry it out. Pray.

If in your married life together you encounter an unforeseen tragedy, you'll need to offer each other extra grace and understanding. Remember, people respond to trauma differently, in their own way and in their own time.

So, rather than pull in or pull away, reach out to your husband, again and again if necessary. And get the help you need from close friends, your church body, and possibly trusted professionals. But above all, know that you can seek comfort and refuge under the wings of God, who tenderly cares for you.

Reflection

- Have you ever experienced tragedy or trauma in your years of marriage?
- Looking back, how did you walk through that experience together? What sorts of things did or would have helped comfort you during that time?

Application

If you've experienced any kind of tragedy, I'm so sorry for what you've been through. Also, I recognize that although we can come through the other side of some traumas (such as I shared above), there are others that change your life forever (which we've also experienced). So let me share a few of my favorite Psalms with the hope that they will comfort you as well.

- "God is our refuge and strength, a very present help in trouble" (Ps. 46:1).
- "This is my comfort in my affliction, that your promise gives me life" (Ps. 119:50).
- "Let your steadfast love comfort me according to your promise to your servant" (Ps. 119:76).

Last, if you're struggling with grief, I recommend the book *A Grace Disguised: How the Soul Grows through Loss* by Jerry Sittser as a helpful, compassionate resource for those walking through death and loss.

Prayer

Oh Father in heaven, my soul cries out to You. I have suffered pain and loss that only You can truly know and understand. Please comfort me—comfort us both—with Your compassionate love. In Jesus's name, amen.

44

Gentleness

> But the wisdom from above is first pure, then peaceable, *gentle*, open to reason, full of mercy and good fruits, impartial and sincere.
>
> James 3:17

Matt and I were definitely having our differences that day. And this wasn't some mild dispute, like over whose turn it was to pick up the kids or who left the stove burner on. No, this disagreement had to do with extended family and, sadly, turned real personal, real quick.

You wouldn't think that an invitation to an upcoming family event could cause such strife, yet there we were staring at each other in the bathroom hall as if the *other* person had a serious problem—and I was convinced it wasn't me. I could go into the details, give you the background, and list each of our compelling reasons, but the bottom line was I didn't think we should go—and Matt did.

Although we agreed to temporarily put the issue aside and carry on with the day, you can believe there was a significant amount of tension between us. I could practically *feel* the friction each time I walked by his chair.

I knew we needed to work it out. Matt and I don't like letting much time go by before we resolve an issue such as this. But the resolution wasn't going to come easy. It would take time and relenting on both our parts—and neither of us was ready to give in right away.

So I reverted to an old favorite when in an argument with him: I ignored him, pretending he wasn't in the same room typing away on his laptop. Like a small child, I made him "invisible," and of course we all know how helpful that is. I'm not saying it's a good or healthy approach, just admitting that this tends to be my impulse when I'm overly upset with him.

But then, about the fifth time I passed my invisible husband in his chair, I abruptly stopped. He looked up, anticipating that I was going to revisit the subject we so strongly disagreed over earlier that day. But he called it wrong, because I gently stroked his face instead.

And, trust me, it must have been Spirit led because it was the last thing I felt like doing at that moment. I *wanted* to argue. I *wanted* to stay angry. So what was with that impulsive gentle touch?

I cannot answer that. But I will tell you that it was a game changer. And by that, I mean his countenance lifted, and my heart softened. With one simple touch, we were both in a significantly better place to work out our differences. Who would've seen that coming?

So, how about you? Have you ever considered the power of a gentle touch in your marriage? A gentle word? You might be surprised at the powerful effect sweet gestures can have on your marriage.

We might mistakenly believe we should reserve our gentleness for the very young or vulnerable—perhaps a child or a frail grandparent—but there's no such distinction found in

Scripture. In fact, in Titus 3:2, we're instructed to always show gentleness "to *all people*" (CSB). Well, that clears things up. There is no distinction of young or old, weak or strong, child or parent or spouse. Your husband counts as among "all people," and so the Bible recommends—no, *instructs*—that you show him gentleness. This doesn't mean saving it only for the good moments; it can also apply to the rougher times.

If you're one who struggles to be gentle—it doesn't come readily or feel necessary to you, or perhaps there's something about expressing gentleness that makes you feel uncomfortably vulnerable—then you can turn to Jesus Christ as your strength and example. He instructs His followers to learn from Him and specifically describes Himself as "gentle and lowly in heart" (Matt. 11:29). As believers, we want to become more and more like Christ, and, friend, He is *gentle.*

So, if this one is a challenge for you, I'd encourage you to go to Jesus. Ask Him to give you a gentle spirit, and see what great things God can do in your marriage with a little gentleness.

Reflection

- Can you think of a time when you were gentle with your husband? What was his response?
- How could you show more gentleness to your husband—with your words, tone, or touch?

Application

Today, as you go about your day, choose one way you want to communicate gentleness to your man. Maybe place a gentle hand on his shoulder, whisper a tender word in his ear, or choose a soft response to a hard conversation. And even if it doesn't come naturally at first or if there isn't an immediate response on his part, keep practicing gentleness and trust God to do the rest.

I hope you'll continue to meditate on and be encouraged by Jesus's words in Matthew 11:29:

> Take my yoke upon you, and learn from me, for I am gentle and lowly in heart, and you will find rest for your souls.

Prayer

Dear Lord, I want to be more like You and be known for my gentle and lowly spirit. Help me to bless our marriage with my gentle words, tone, and touch. In Jesus's name, amen.

45

Money

For where your treasure is, there your heart will be also.

Matthew 6:21

The doctor occasionally referred to her as our "million-dollar baby."

Initially, I wasn't exactly sure what he meant by that and, frankly, was afraid to ask. Our fifth child suffered a stroke before birth, and it would be a long time before anyone would know what that might mean for her life. However, there was one thing the NICU pediatrician was confident of: If our daughter lived, she would be one very expensive baby.

Still in shock, her dad and I could hardly bear to think in such terms, let alone plan for them. But that's okay because Dr. NICU was already thinking for us. He predicted we would have a long, hard road ahead of us, and he wasn't speaking only in medical terms.

We would undoubtedly be facing severe financial pressure.

Perhaps you can relate to some of what I'm saying here. Although you may not have a child with severe special needs, maybe you've experienced your own unforeseen circumstances that have weighed you down—even threatened your marriage— and taken their toll. And you know how easily financial struggles can turn into financial strife.

If this is your situation, then let me gently remind you that you and your husband are on the same team—even more than that, in God's eyes, the two of you are as *one* (Eph. 5:31). No matter what money problems or challenges you're up against, determine right now to face them together. Don't let the Enemy use this already difficult hardship to divide you further.

Then, if I could add one more caution here: Resist the temptation to turn on the other person and accuse them (either loudly or silently) of something they should have done, or should *not* have done, under the circumstances. Not that you should avoid having a hard conversation when necessary, but make it your marriage goal to go forward together as much as possible.

Next, while there are a number of practical resources (budgets, books, financial counseling, etc.) I could mention that might be of great help, don't forget that God invites us to lay all our concerns before Him. He is our Heavenly Father, and He cares about our needs, so don't take a "we got ourselves into this, so we'll have to get ourselves out" approach. Instead, as a child of God, take it before Him in prayer.

Last, rather than becoming consumed with the financial hurdle before you, choose to find things for which you can be thankful too. Instead of staring at that staggering bill from the local hospital, Matt and I wanted to focus on the fact that, by God's grace, our daughter lived in spite of her grave injuries. And we could rejoice that she brings us joy every day of her life. We have so much for which to be grateful that has nothing to do with finances.

So, I don't know what your situation might be—if you've lost a job, can't get work, have health issues, or have unplanned expenses. Or it's possible that you simply haven't handled your finances wisely. Whatever the case may be—as my husband often reminds me—this might not be what you had planned, but none of this comes as a surprise to God.

He knows our troubles and has good intentions toward us. And we know that He wants us to walk in love together above all.

Reflection

- Are you and your husband on the same page regarding money and finances?
- How do the two of you face financial hardships or deal with budget decisions?

Application

You might be surprised how many times the Bible addresses money and the place it has in our lives (and hearts). Although it might seem more like a subject for modern times, it's a topic that's been around since near the beginning of time. I'd suggest spending the next few days studying what Scripture says about "treasure." Here are a handful of verses from both the Old and New Testaments (and this is only a "starter" list—there are many more!): Proverbs 13:1; 22:1, 7; Ecclesiastes 5:10; Matthew 6:24; Luke 12:15; 1 Timothy 6:10; and Hebrews 13:5.

Next, take out your notebook and divide a page into two columns. On the left side, label the column "What the world says," and on the right side, label it "What God's Word says." Then, as you go through these verses and others, write down both the world's and God's perspectives on each.

If it's been a while since you and your husband have discussed your budget or financial needs, initiate setting aside a time in the next few weeks for a healthy, and hopefully helpful, conversation. Just be sure you communicate that you want to be a positive part of the process and that you wish to be a unified team.

Prayer

Dear Lord, I desire that our lives be "free from love of money" (Heb. 13:5) and that we will be content with what we have. Help us have a godly perspective of our financial situation and make wise decisions about how we handle our money. In Jesus's name, amen.

46

Faithfulness

So they are no longer two but one flesh. What therefore God has joined together, let not man separate.

Matthew 19:6

A few years back, my husband began working closely with one particular woman who gave me cause for more than a little concern. She shared openly with Matt about her troubled marriage and impending divorce. And another red flag: This woman was both intelligent and interesting—two very attractive qualities to a man like my husband.

So, after carefully praying over the matter for nearly a week, I approached Matt and said something like, "I know you love me and are committed to God and our marriage. And while I can't imagine you'd ever have a 'real' affair, I worry about an *emotional* affair. And *if* you were ever to be tempted by another woman . . . it would be her."

We'd been married for over ten years by then, but it was our first conversation of this type, so, naturally, I waited anxiously for how he'd respond. Finally, after a few quiet minutes, he answered, "You're right. On both accounts. I would never be unfaithful to you, but if it could happen . . . it would be someone like her."

Following this sobering acknowledgment, I then pointed out that even if *he* wasn't at risk, what about her? Was it fair to her to be working so closely together with him when she was in such a vulnerable place? What about *her* heart?

He admitted he hadn't looked at the situation from that perspective—he was truly just trying to be kind to her by offering a sympathetic ear—but he could see my point. And so we talked about what should happen next. On the one hand, we both genuinely cared for this Christian sister and didn't want to hurt or disappoint her. But on the other hand, it was vital we protect our marriage.

And it was with that intention that Matt purposed to pull back on how closely he and this woman worked together. He also gently let her know that she'd need to find another Christian friend or counselor with whom to discuss her personal life and that he was very sorry, but he could no longer be that person in whom she confided.

I'm not positive she fully understood the reason for these changes in their working relationship, but she did respect us for it. And for that, I'm grateful.

Now, if at this point, you're wondering if I was possibly overreacting to the situation, let's remember that most affairs *begin* as casual friendships, so my concern wasn't totally unfounded. Furthermore, the older Matt and I get and the more moral tragedies we hear about, the more we see that earlier situation as having been a close call. Possibly even closer than we realized at the time.

To be clear, it's not that I'm against any friendships with the opposite sex. On the contrary, Matt and I both enjoy many different friendships and working relationships. We don't live in a bubble, nor do we want to. But most everyone who knows us well also knows that we're careful about avoiding the kind of intimacy that might lead to any sort of adultery—sexual or emotional. We are committed to protecting the *purity* and the *oneness* in our marriage.

As believers, we don't want to lose sight of Scripture's warning that we are to be "sober-minded" and "watchful" because we have an enemy who "prowls around like a roaring lion, seeking someone to devour" (1 Pet. 5:8). So, while we don't need to overreact or be overly suspicious, we shouldn't ignore this biblical caution to be alert and watchful.

Being watchful might mean identifying a potentially risky relationship developing with you or your spouse. Being sober-minded might mean setting up healthy boundaries or protective policies. That's between you and your husband. But one thing I know is that our marriage—*your* marriage—is something sacred and worth protecting.

Reflection

- Are you and your husband proactive about protecting your marriage?
- Have the two of you conversed about how you would address concerns should any come up?

Application

As a Christian wife, do you embrace the idea of complete faithfulness in marriage? Not only with your body but with your thoughts and affections? Or are you giving pieces of your heart to anyone other than your husband? And, to be sure, the standard should be the same for both spouses.

So, if you haven't done so already, purpose to sit down and have a candid conversation with your husband about protecting your marriage. Talk about the *why* as well as what this might mean for you. Remember, protecting your marriage is about being *wise*, not fearful. Then work together to set up reasonable boundaries and protections that you can both agree on. For us, that includes not spending extensive one-on-one time or counseling (formally or informally) with someone of the opposite sex, but you'll have your own set of policies that work best for your marriage.

Prayer

Dear Heavenly Father, I want there to be nothing but complete faithfulness in our marriage. Please give us discernment in how we can wisely protect our love and commitment to one another. Help us to be unified in our approach to relationships outside of our marriage, that they would be healthy, pure, and appropriate. In Jesus's name, amen.

47

Comfort

Blessed be the God and Father of our Lord Jesus Christ, the Father of mercies and God of all comfort, who comforts us in all our affliction, so that we may be able to comfort those who are in any affliction, with the comfort with which we ourselves are comforted by God.

2 Corinthians 1:3–4

We all cried the day Matt's dad died. It didn't matter that we had long known this day was coming or even that we realized it was more of a mercy by then. My father-in-law had been suffering from a serious heart condition for many years and, by the end of his time, he was ready to be free from his failing body and go home to his Savior at last.

Yet still, we couldn't stop the tears, aching over the empty place he left in our lives.

But no one felt it more than Matt. Not only had he lost a father—he had lost his best friend. Early every morning for over twenty years, Matt walked next door so the two of them could have coffee together while they discussed the news, talked politics, exchanged ideas, and shared dreams. So you can imagine the tremendous hole that was left after Dad departed.

Matt grieved deeply, and I longed to comfort him.

However, when it comes to grief, my husband has a hard time letting anyone in, even me. I learned this about him in our first few years of marriage and, being young and not knowing what else to do, I gave him space since that was what he desired. In those days, I believed it to be the loving thing to do. But I don't think that way anymore.

My perspective changed when I came across a familiar Bible passage—2 Corinthians 1:3–4, where God instructs us to comfort one another—and it seemed as though I was seeing it for the first time. As I read these verses, I thought back to our many trials and heartaches over the years and how we had experienced the sustaining grace that God alone can give through it all. He is truly "the Father of mercies and God of all comfort" (v. 3).

Perhaps you've experienced this kind of indescribable comfort as well—that sense of being wrapped tight in the arms of Him "who comforts us in all our affliction" (v. 4). You've been upheld by the God of all comfort.

But there's more. Returning to that first chapter in 2 Corinthians, we see the passage doesn't stop with God's comfort for us—it goes on to say that it's *because* of the comfort we've known that we can comfort others as well. We have experienced something beautiful, and now we're to pass on the same to others. We have something to do.

Another interesting insight into this passage is that the word *comfort* in the Greek (*parakaleō*) can also mean "to call to one's side" or "to call near."[1] So, with this added definition, we learn that comfort is about *doing* something, but it is also about *being* something. *Comfort* means someone who is near.

Now, for me and our marriage, it might mean sticking close to my husband, not leaving his side when he's sad or mourning. For your marriage, comfort might call for something else—perhaps a gentle hug, a word of sympathy, or sitting nearby so your husband knows he's not walking through his sorrow alone—not if you can help it.

But maybe you're the one who is longing to be comforted and your husband isn't offering much. It's possible he is uncomfortable or doesn't know what to do. You could try sitting down with him and sharing a few simple things he could do to help you walk through this time. Tell him it would mean a lot to you if he would listen as you process your grief or if he would hold you while you cry or maybe just quietly hand you a box of tissues. Let him know that you don't expect him to "fix" anything but simply to stay by your side.

Lean in and let your grief be something that only brings your hearts closer together.

Reflection

- Do you find it natural to offer comfort to your husband? Or is it a challenge?
- How do you think your husband would best receive comfort from you?

Application

I think you'll be encouraged by the many verses that say how God comforts us in our time of need. You might want to write each one out in your notebook or pick out a favorite one to memorize.

- "Even though I walk through the valley of the shadow of death, I will fear no evil, for you are with me; your rod and your staff, they comfort me" (Ps. 23:4).
- "This is my comfort in my affliction, that your promise gives me life" (Ps. 119:50).
- "Let your steadfast love comfort me according to your promise to your servant" (Ps. 119:76).
- "Blessed are those who mourn, for they shall be comforted" (Matt. 5:4).

Prayer

Dear Heavenly Father, thank You for Your comfort throughout my many trials and grief. As You have brought me comfort, I want to be a source of comfort to my husband as well. Help me also to clearly communicate what I need from him in this time. In Jesus's name, amen.

48

Rest

And he said to them, "Come away by yourselves to a desolate place and rest a while." For many were coming and going, and they had no leisure even to eat.

Mark 6:31

'll confess I was astonished when Matt announced that he and I would take the day off on that particular Friday. I was bewildered because we've always worked on Fridays. We've homeschooled our kids on Fridays. We've taken care of our sweet girl who has special needs on Fridays. So how could we suddenly be all irresponsible and skip out on a Friday?

It felt a little crazy, but I did what I could to clear the schedule, and he did the same on his end. We canceled appointments, arranged for the boys' schooling, and lined up a caregiver for Avonléa. And I quietly hoped that whatever he had in mind would be worth this gigantic effort.

It was worth it, all right.

Because after driving several hours through the barren but beautiful landscape of Eastern Oregon, we spent a glorious day soaking in a natural hot spring. And we never do stuff like this. Like you, we never feel as though we *can* do things like this—too many responsibilities and too much to do.

But that turned out to be only the beginning. Matt also declared that from now on, we'd try to set aside Fridays as our "Sabbath day." This would be the one day (Sundays don't really "count" when you're a pastor) when we would stop our work, close our laptops, turn off our phones, and *rest*.

Now, maybe the necessity of rest is evident to you and you're wondering what took us so long to realize it. Good question. We had always embraced the concept of regular rest and counseled countless people to make it a priority, and yet we struggled to put it into practice for ourselves. Always one more thing to do, one more project to finish, or one more need to meet. So we kept pressing on like a couple of hamsters running on a continuous wheel.

Until at last, we stopped to realize how dearly we were paying for our hamster-wheel lifestyle. Our health was suffering, and our spirits were weary. And if we didn't do something, we were going to suffer grave consequences. Possibly burnout.

So Friday it is. "As good as therapy," I only half joked to Matt as we enjoyed one of our recent Sabbath getaways. "Less expensive too."

Although I might have spoken lightly in the moment, this intentional rest has seriously done wonders for our bodies, minds, and souls. And it's been like a long drink of cool water for our marriage.

This day of rest has given us the time to enjoy actual conversation that consists of more than problem-solving or decision-making. It's enabled us to do things together outside of normal duties. Plus, without so much noise and distraction, we can really hear each other again.

Now, it might be that you're in a season where rest feels like a luxury. Trust me; we've been there! Perhaps you're looking after a newborn or several young children, are in the middle of a big move or job change, or are caring for aging parents or someone who is chronically ill. Even in those challenging situations, it's essential you step away in any small way you can.

In case you're not entirely convinced, let's look at the example of Jesus Himself:

> And he [Jesus] said to them [the disciples], "Come away by yourselves to a desolate place and rest a while." For many were coming and going, and they had no leisure even to eat. And they went away in the boat to a desolate place by themselves. (Mark 6:31–32)

I'd say three things stand out to me in that short story. The first is the phrase *come away*, as in get *away* from the hustle and bustle. The second is simply the word *rest*, which is to say, *stop* moving and working so you can recover your strength! But the third is my personal favorite as the mother of eight children: "They had no leisure even to eat." Don't you know that feeling?

So, friend, let me encourage you to make time for rest. If not for a whole day, then block off several hours here or there—it might be the best thing you can do for yourself and your marriage right now.

Reflection

- Do you and your husband have time set aside each week to rest? Part of a day? An evening?
- What would feel restful to you right now in the season you're currently in?

Application

While we touched on Jesus's own example of resting in the book of Mark (and there are others), the Bible offers many other verses on the topic. Consider these verses, and then make a short note in your notebook of what each one says about resting: Psalm 46:10; 127:2; Proverbs 3:24; and Matthew 11:28.

The next step is probably the hardest: Decide *when* you will rest. Study your schedule and see if there are any habits or activities you can cancel or remove to make room for this priority. And if you can't see a way, ask your husband or a good friend to evaluate your calendar for you. Sometimes a commitment we consider essential is actually optional and would be better replaced by rest.

Prayer

Dear Heavenly Father, I want to be still and know You are God (Ps. 46:10). Help me to see where and how we can find rest in the middle of this busy season. Renew our love and restore our strength in the joy of resting in You. In Jesus's name, amen.

49

Mercy

For judgment is without mercy to one who has shown no mercy. Mercy triumphs over judgment.

James 2:13

It's not often I watch my husband weep. But there we were, snuggled together on a Saturday night, when a song came on—a beautiful ballad unfamiliar to either of us. So I was surprised to see tears start in his eyes and stream down his dear face. I was mystified by what could have moved him so.

The tune and the lyrics were relatively simple yet somehow stirring all the same—the singer always returning to that one line: "We all could use a little mercy now." *A little mercy, please.* Yet it was that final refrain that touched us most—the part about how we might not deserve it . . . "but *we need it anyhow.*"[1]

And so, it was this mournful ballad that made me realize I'd never looked at that man next to me as someone who might need mercy. Somehow I had always expected him to stay strong and, unconsciously, even held him to a higher standard. Inwardly I believed there was less room for mistakes for the man of the family. But he wouldn't have wept at that song if it hadn't struck a chord deep inside his soul.

Evidently, my husband was longing for mercy—a show of compassion—and now I was left to wonder why he hadn't received more from me. More grace for mistakes, more clemency for offenses, more room to grow. The kind of mercy I wanted him to have for me.

Perhaps you have the gift of mercy, and it comes naturally for you. For many of us, however, it is something we must choose and doesn't necessarily sit right with us. *Why should we let him get away with it when he's done wrong or disappointed us in some way? Why should he not pay the price for his failings?* The very idea of offering mercy in such a situation goes smack against our sense of justice.

But then again, as believers, we must acknowledge the prominent place mercy is given throughout the Bible. For instance, Jesus directly instructs us in the book of Luke, "Be merciful, even as your Father is merciful" (6:36). And, in the Beatitudes, He tells us, "Blessed are the merciful, for they shall receive mercy" (Matt. 5:7). But I think my favorite mercy verse is the one in James that says, "Mercy triumphs over judgment" (2:13). How sobering to think that when it comes to relationships—yes, including our marriage relationship—mercy must have the last word.

Mercy triumphs over judgment. That is to say, mercy always wins.

So, while you might be familiar with the general definition of *mercy*, let's consider the biblical meaning as well. The word in Greek is *eleos* and is defined as "kindness or good will towards the miserable and the afflicted, joined with a desire to help them."[2] Doesn't the idea of showing kindness "towards the miserable" tug at your heart a bit? It does mine.

Then there's the last phrase in the definition, the part about desiring "to help them." Mercy isn't merely expressing sympathy or shrugging to let your husband off the hook—it's intentionally helping out your soul mate, whether or not he deserves it or asks for it. Mercy isn't giving in or giving up; it's actively reaching out your hand to someone who needs your help and compassion.

So, friend, maybe your husband could use a little mercy too. Because we all could.

Reflection

- Do you have the gift of mercy? How do you show mercy to others?
- In what way could your husband "use a little mercy" from you?

Application

If you find it difficult to be merciful toward your husband, consider spending a few minutes reflecting on God's mercies. Both the Old and New Testaments are replete with verses reminding us of how great His mercy is toward us:

- "The LORD is merciful and gracious, slow to anger and abounding in steadfast love" (Ps. 103:8).
- "The steadfast love of the LORD never ceases; his mercies never come to an end; they are new every morning; great is your faithfulness" (Lam. 3:22–23).
- "But God, being rich in mercy, because of the great love with which he loved us, even when we were dead in

our trespasses, made us alive together with Christ—by grace you have been saved" (Eph. 2:4–5).

- "Let us then with confidence draw near to the throne of grace, that we may receive mercy and find grace to help in time of need" (Heb. 4:16).

As you study these verses (and more), begin writing the specific ways God has shown mercy to you. If you didn't do it earlier in this devotional, include your personal testimony of salvation, as well as the many instances when He has been merciful in your time of need.

Then (drying your tears if necessary), contemplate how your husband might need mercy from you. For example, have you judged him harshly? Has there been a time when you withheld your kindness because, in your view, he didn't warrant it? Ask God to soften your heart and show some mercy.

Prayer

Dear Heavenly Father, these Scripture verses remind me that Your mercies are made "new every morning" (Lam. 3:23) and that You "help in time of need" (Heb. 4:16). I confess I haven't been very merciful toward my husband, but I want to change that now. Give me a compassionate heart and a desire to help him. In Jesus's name, amen.

50

Self-Control

For God gave us a spirit not of fear but of power and love and self-control.

2 Timothy 1:7

First of all, the incident occurred on a Sunday morning—on *Sunday* of all days—and during our coffee time of all *times*. Naturally. Not on a Tuesday or a Thursday or conveniently on a Saturday when we might have the leisure to work it out right then and there.

No, the offensive remark was made on a Sunday morning and, what's worse, it was made by my pastor-husband. The day had begun so beautifully too, with warm sunshine and worship music filling the house, doughnuts from the bakery, and several pots of hot coffee. But then, just as we were ready to break and do the mad dash to prepare for church, he had to go and say it.

"Okay, boys, looks like this is all your mom is serving for breakfast, so let's have at it." And he threw it out to our sons as though I wasn't sitting *right there.*

I believe those are more or less the words he used. What he meant by them, however (as he explained later), was something straightforward like, "Let's finish up the last of these doughnuts and get a move on to dress for church."

But here's the barb I thought I heard: "Well, sons, it appears your mom doesn't know how to cook a proper breakfast for growing boys, so I guess we'll have to settle for sugar and carbs this morning." (Is that what you heard too?)

And I found his remark hurtful and humiliating. Further compounded by the fact that I'd been up since early that morning doing *other things* to get our family ready for church.

Thank you, Pastor Matt.

Now, what do you do when you're hurt and offended? Me, I rarely cry or retreat; I'm far more likely to get mad—and *fiery mad* when it's by my husband. So, although I refrained from saying anything in the moment in front of the children, I began furiously rehearsing my follow-up remarks in response to his cutting comment once I was back in our bedroom.

Yet then, out of nowhere, something interrupted my mutterings—possibly thanks to the worship music or the thought of the church service we were preparing for—and I slowly settled down to have a frank talk with myself.

It went something like this:

"Lisa, so you found his comment offensive, but will it go well to address this topic right now as you're rushing off to church? Is it a good time? Will there be enough time?"

No, no, and no.

And still, the conversation continued.

"Lisa, is your husband a pastor?"

Obviously.

"And will it help this man you love—even as upset as you are right now—to lay into him *before* he gets ready to teach the church body this morning? Or do you think you can hold off?"

I didn't need to answer that one. I knew it could wait; I just didn't want it to.

But wouldn't you know it, I'd been studying self-control (of all things!) the previous week, and here was my chance to practice it. *Lucky me.* A made-to-order opportunity to rein in my (angry) passions. So I called out to God right then and there to help calm my fury.

Now, I can't say all my hurt and angry emotions instantly disappeared—yet, strangely, rather than feeling constrained by my decision to wait, I felt surprisingly free. My rage didn't have the power to determine *how* and *when* we'd have this discussion; it felt good to know that it was for me to decide.

Here, I have a confession to make: I hesitated to share this story. I'm ashamed of my struggle with self-control and the fact that I still wrestle with anger, even after all these years. But maybe you have your own issues with self-control that very few people know about. Perhaps not with anger; possibly you battle with healthy eating, screen time, your speech, sexual temptation, or other areas in your life. And you, too, have been hesitant for anyone to know this part of your story.

That's because the Enemy wants you to believe that you are alone in your struggle. *But you are not.*

And he wants to convince you that you are helpless in your situation. *But you are not.*

Oh friend, you are *not* on your own at all; however, it might feel the exact opposite. When we *walk* in the Spirit, when *filled* with the Spirit, we have power over our flesh and temptations. With God's help, we *can* control ourselves and enjoy the surprising freedom found in the restraint.

Reflection

- What is an area of your life that you struggle to control?
- Have you believed the lie that you are alone or helpless in your struggle? What is the truth found in Scripture?

Application

I encourage you to pray over the area with which you've been struggling. Ask God to help you, to show how you might walk in victory. And don't forget the truth of what He says in His Word—that He "gave us a spirit not of fear but of power and love and *self-control*" (2 Tim. 1:7). Maybe you'll want to write out the verse and post it where you'll need it most. You might also want to invite a trustworthy friend or counselor to support and pray for you.

If you're interested in further study on self-control, here are some more verses for you to reflect upon: Proverbs 25:28; 1 Corinthians 9:27; 10:13; and 1 Peter 4:7.

Prayer

Dear Lord, I want to remember You've given me a spirit of self-control, and the truth is I can master my passions. So fill me with Your Spirit and help me walk in the Spirit, that I might not be at the mercy of my natural impulses. In Jesus's name, amen.

51

Perseverance

And let us not grow weary while doing good, for in due season we shall reap if we do not lose heart.

Galatians 6:9 NKJV

Our youngest daughter never did learn to walk. Because of a stroke she suffered before birth, our darling girl lost the use of both her legs and most of her left arm. And yet our Avonléa remains a little trouper, and there's not much that gets her down. She motors around in her wheelchair and is rather adept at pulling herself across the floor when necessary, moving in her own version of a one-armed military-style crawl. She may not travel too fast, but that girl gets the job done.

Except for those stairs going up to her bedroom—they are a tremendous challenge for someone like her. And why wouldn't they be? After all, how does a child who's limited to one arm climb an entire flight of stairs? That's the question that increasingly weighed on us—and it's the challenge her father took head-on.

Nearly every day, as soon as she was old enough to try, her daddy gave her stair-climbing lessons. Slowly and persistently, he guided her up those first few steps, having her reach with her one strong right arm and then *pull, pull, pull*. Over and over again.

And, oh, she hated every minute of it. How she howled and complained! It's not that the exercise caused her any pain; it's just that it was so very hard. *Impossible* is how I would have described it, and, more than once, I implored my husband to quit. Clearly, she wasn't making any progress, and given her disabilities, it was doubtful that she ever would.

But still, he wouldn't give up.

Then one day, when she was twelve years old, I looked up from the living room couch and realized our Avonléa was on the fifth step—all on her own. Astonished, I shrieked, and my shout brought the rest of the family running into the room. Standing together at the bottom of the stairs, we simultaneously cheered and cried as she slowly pulled herself up—*pull, pull, pull*—to the very top step. We watched as our miracle girl made history right before our eyes!

After seven years of stair-climbing lessons with no sign of improvement or reason to hope, our daughter had suddenly conquered those stairs.

I say "suddenly" because that's how it felt on that day, and yet that wouldn't be taking into account the seven years of relentless effort that came before. The story behind her wild success was largely due to my husband's willingness to persevere—despite the odds or lack of visible progress.

But our story is not the only one. Perhaps you, too, know what it's like to try something for a long time without apparent results, and maybe you feel as though you've been climbing and climbing without ever getting anywhere. You don't see much (or any) forward motion, and you're ready to give up.

I understand that feeling. I think we've all experienced situations or seasons in which we've longed to give up or give in. It's a normal part of the Christian life, and it can be the case for the Christian marriage as well. I don't say this to minimize what you're going through but to encourage you that you're not alone in your experience. I doubt there's a single couple who can't point back to a time when perseverance was required in their marriage—a time to stick it out, to press forward, to *pull, pull, pull.*

So, friend, I hope you won't grow weary of doing good. That you will *persevere.* You never know what God is going to do in your marriage. He sees your faithfulness, your willingness to try and to keep trying. Your loving efforts are not lost on Him.

Reflection

- Is there an area in your marriage that you've been working on, seemingly without making much progress?
- If so, are you willing to persevere through it? What does *enduring* mean in your particular situation?

Application

Sometimes if you're struggling to persevere in a situation, it can be helpful to write out what it is you're working toward or hoping for, detailing as many specifics as possible. Then you might try listing the potential rewards of pressing on in your marriage: for example, a closer relationship, a deeper understanding, and a lasting union.

I can also recommend asking a close friend or family member to pray for you and perhaps "cheer" for you as well. Who doesn't need a bit of encouraging cheer when they're feeling weary or discouraged? We all do.

Finally, here are some more questions for your study of what the Bible says about the believer and perseverance:

- What is promised to the person "who remains steadfast under trial" (James 1:12)?
- What does the Bible say we will reap if we do not give up (Gal. 6:8–9)?
- According to Romans 5:3–5, what does endurance produce?
- What is described as the "full effect" of steadfastness (James 1:4)?

Prayer

Dear Lord, I want to be a woman who perseveres, someone who does not easily give up. Help me press on in Your strength and remember that You are working in ways that I cannot yet see. In Jesus's name, amen.

52

Gospel

For I am not ashamed of the gospel, for it is the power of God for salvation to everyone who believes, to the Jew first and also to the Greek.

Romans 1:16

Our flight attendant was probably trying her best, but you couldn't miss the edge in her voice as she made her way down the narrow airplane aisle, rattling off instructions we'd all heard countless times before.

Not that I blamed her for her monotone. It was a night flight, and I think nearly every one of us felt *done* right from the start. So many tired people squeezed into such a small space, most of us just wanting to get home and get to bed.

My heart went out to her, and I did what I could to win her over, smiling warmly as she passed our row, but no luck there. I thanked her for the plastic bottle of water, later adding a polite "excuse me" while inching my way around her to reach the restroom. Yet the woman remained visibly irritable from takeoff to landing.

You could practically hear the collective sigh of relief when the plane touched the ground at last. Matt and I gladly grabbed our carry-ons and started to head off the plane when the attendant stopped us just before we reached the door. She pulled me off to one side, whispering that she had something to say to me. Tired and confused, I couldn't think of what I possibly could have done to warrant a pull-over such as this.

There I waited at the front of the plane to hear whatever grievance our grumpy attendant might have against me. But I'd misjudged the situation. She didn't have a complaint; she had a question. A little haltingly at first, she asked softly, "Do you mind if I ask . . . what you two are celebrating?" And, for the first time that evening, I saw the young woman venture a smile.

I was rather unprepared for her question and didn't have an answer. How could I tell her we weren't really celebrating anything? That we were merely flying home from a *Focus on the Family* interview and were eager to return to our family.

"Celebrating? Oh, I don't know; *love*, I guess. We're just loving each other." I shrugged.

I could've kicked myself. Why couldn't I have come up with a better response than that? Never thought to mention that we'd been married for nearly thirty years or that we had eight children or to say a single word about the faithfulness of God! Such an awkward answer.

She appeared to appreciate my reply nonetheless. As if this simple "loving each other" was somehow better than a second honeymoon or an important anniversary. There we were, just an older married couple holding hands and sharing tiny airplane pretzels. Talking, laughing, snuggling. Nothing too special. Without a thought that we might be observed.

But someone *was* paying attention. And it was a good reminder that you never know who might be watching—and what might whisper a word of hope to someone who desperately needs it.

So whether you're mindful of it or not, your marriage is sending out a message. The way you communicate your love for one another—that visible display of affection, kindness, joy—says a lot about the God you serve. For some people, it might be the only sermon they ever hear. Or at least listen to.

It's a fact. Your marriage has tremendous power to preach the gospel to everyone around you, and that's just what God intended! Your outward expressions of love for each other are an unmistakable testimony of what He has done and continues to do in your life. You don't have to say a thing; they "hear" the gospel by viewing your relationship.

> By this all people will know that you are my disciples, if you have love for one another. (John 13:35)

Reflection

- Have you ever considered your marriage as a gospel message to those around you?
- How would you describe the "message" of your relationship with your husband?

Application

First, take a few minutes to reflect on what is meant by *the gospel*. You might even want to write it out for future reference, highlighting the words or phrases that stand out to you.

The *Wycliffe Bible Encyclopedia* summarizes the gospel this way:

> The central truth of the gospel is that God has provided a way of salvation for men through the gift of His son to the world. He suffered as a sacrifice for sin, overcame death, and now offers a share in His triumph to all who will accept it. The gospel is good news because it is a gift of God, not something that must be earned by penance or by self-improvement (Jn. 3:16; Rom. 5:8–11; II Cor. 5:14–19; Tit. 2:11–14).[1]

Next, list the many different ways your marriage can reflect the Good News of Jesus Christ. For example, here are a few ideas that come to my mind:

- When I show kindness to my husband, I give others a small glimpse of the kindness that's been shown to me.
- When my husband and I offer grace to one another, we are a testimony of the grace God has given us.
- The joy we take in one another reflects the joy we experience knowing Christ Jesus as our Lord and Savior.

Can you come up with any other mini-sermons for your own marriage preaching? The possibilities are endless!

Prayer

Dear Heavenly Father, I'm grateful for Your merciful gift of salvation. As others watch our marriage, I hope that above all—even with our mistakes and imperfections—they will see Your love shining through us. And that they will be drawn to You. In Jesus's name, amen.

Closing Note

My Dear Friend,

I'm genuinely grateful for how we've been able to spend this last year together, searching the Scriptures and discussing so many beautiful and often deeply personal topics together. I imagine it hasn't always been easy to find the time, let alone the will, to do the hard work of studying, stretching, healing, and sometimes surrendering. But I do hope, upon looking back, that you've found it to be a truly fruitful endeavor—and that the Lord will richly bless your life and marriage in the years to come.

In His grace,
Lisa Jacobson

Notes

Week 12 Respect

1. "G5091, timaō," Strong's Greek Lexicon (ESV), Blue Letter Bible, accessed March 22, 2022, https://www.blueletterbible.org/lexicon/g5091/esv/mgnt/0-1/.

Week 17 Granting Forgiveness

1. "G5483, charizomai," Strong's Greek Lexicon (ESV), Blue Letter Bible, accessed March 22, 2022, https://www.blueletterbible.org/lexicon/g5483/esv/mgnt/0-1/.

Week 27 Kindness

1. Lisa Jacobson and Phylicia Masonheimer, *The Flirtation Experiment: Putting Magic, Mystery, and Spark into Your Everyday Marriage* (Nashville: Thomas Nelson, 2021), 19–22.

Week 29 Hope

1. "G1411, dynamis," Strong's Greek Lexicon (ESV), Blue Letter Bible, accessed March 22, 2022, https://www.blueletterbible.org/lexicon/g1411/esv/mgnt/0-1/.

Week 32 Purity

1. Freedom Course, https://www.faithfullife.com/freedom-course.

Week 34 Worship

1. "H7812, šāḥâ," Strong's Hebrew Lexicon (ESV), Blue Letter Bible, accessed March 22, 2022, https://www.blueletterbible.org/lexicon/h7812/esv/wlc/0-1/.

2. "G4352, proskyneō," Strong's Greek Lexicon (ESV), Blue Letter Bible, accessed March 22, 2022, https://www.blueletterbible.org/lexicon/g4352/esv/mgnt/0-1/.

Week 36 Holiness

1. "G40, hagios," Strong's Greek Lexicon (ESV), Blue Letter Bible, accessed March 22, 2022, https://www.blueletterbible.org/lexicon/g40/esv/mgnt/0-1/.

2. "G3956, pas," Strong's Greek Lexicon (ESV), Blue Letter Bible, accessed March 22, 2022, https://www.blueletterbible.org/lexicon/g3956/esv/mgnt/0-1/.

3. "G391, anastrophē," Strong's Greek Lexicon (ESV), Blue Letter Bible, accessed March 22, 2022, https://www.blueletterbible.org/lexicon/g391/esv/mgnt/0-1/.

Week 37 Grace

1. "G5485, charis," Strong's Greek Lexicon (ESV), Blue Letter Bible, accessed March 22, 2022, https://www.blueletterbible.org/lexicon/g5485/esv/mgnt/0-1/.

2. "G741, artyō," Strong's Greek Lexicon (ESV), Blue Letter Bible, accessed March 22, 2022, https://www.blueletterbible.org/lexicon/g741/esv/mgnt/0-1/.

Week 42 Submission

1. "G5293, hypotassō," Strong's Greek Lexicon (ESV), Blue Letter Bible, accessed March 22, 2022, https://www.blueletterbible.org/lexicon/g5293/esv/mgnt/0-1/.

2. "G5293, hupotasso," *Vine's Expository Dictionary of New Testament Words*, Blue Letter Bible, accessed March 22, 2022, https://www.blueletterbible.org/search/dictionary/viewtopic.cfm?topic=VT0002826.

3. "G5293, hypotassō," Strong's Greek Lexicon (ESV), accessed March 22, 2022.

Week 47 Comfort

1. "G3870, parakaleō," Strong's Greek Lexicon (ESV), Blue Letter Bible, accessed March 22, 2022, https://www.blueletterbible.org/lexicon/g3870/esv/mgnt/0-1/?.

Week 49 Mercy

1. "Mercy Now," track 2 on Mary Gauthier, *Mercy Now*, Lost Highway, 2005.

2. "G1656, eleos," Strong's Greek Lexicon (ESV), Blue Letter Bible, accessed March 22, 2022, https://www.blueletterbible.org/lexicon/g1656/esv/mgnt/0-1/.

Week 52 Gospel

1. Charles F. Pfeiffer, *Wycliffe Bible Encyclopedia* (Chicago: Moody Press, 1975).

Lisa Jacobson is an author, a speaker, and the founder and host of Club31Women.com, an online community of Christian women authors. She is the author of the bestselling *100 Ways to Love Your Husband* and *100 Words of Affirmation Your Husband Needs to Hear*. A graduate of Western Seminary, Lisa lives with her husband, Matt, in the Pacific Northwest, where they have raised their eight children. Together Matt and Lisa are cohosts of the popular *Faithful Life* podcast.

Hands-On Advice
to *LOVE* Your Spouse Better

Simple, Powerful Action Steps to
Love Your Child Well

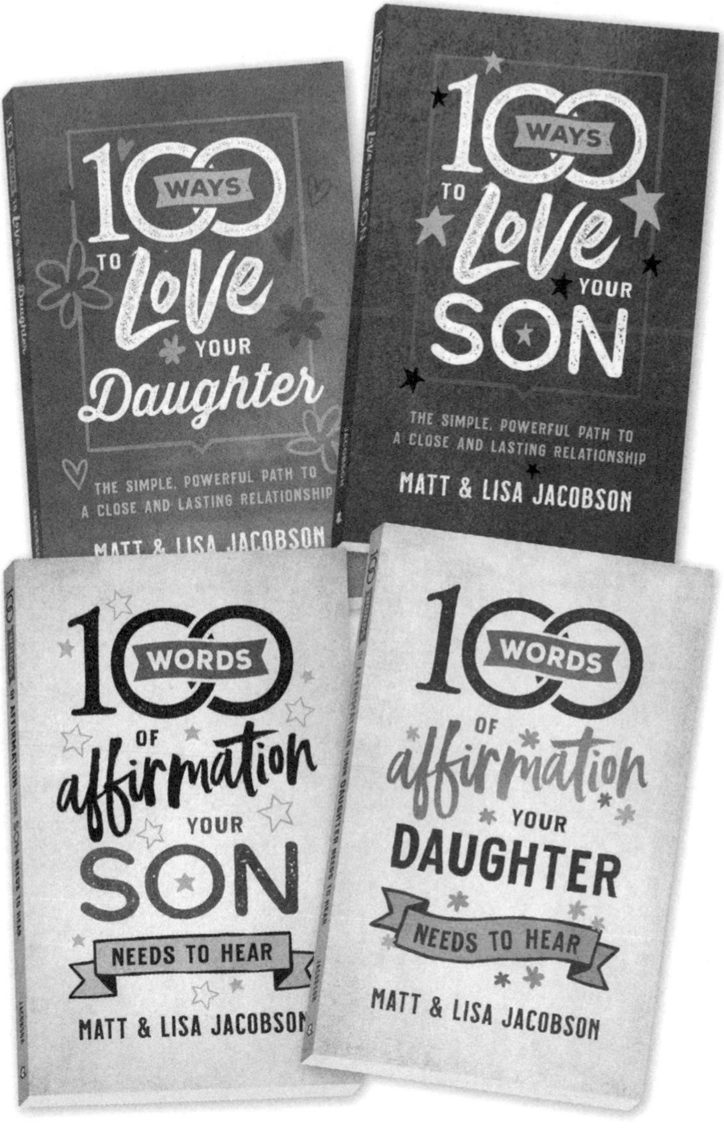

Connect with
Lisa and *Club31Women!*

Club31Women.com

Cohost of the *FAITHFUL LIFE* Podcast

Follow Along @Club31Women